Changing
Special Education
Now

Open University Press
Children With Special Needs Series

Editors

PHILLIP WILLIAMS
Emeritus Professor of Education
University College of North Wales, Bangor.

PETER YOUNG
Formerly Tutor in the education of children with
learning difficulties, Cambridge Institute of Education;
educational writer, researcher and consultant.

This is a series of short and authoritative introductions for parents, teachers, professionals and anyone concerned with children with special needs. The series will cover the range of physical, sensory, mental, emotional and behavioural difficulties, and the changing needs from infancy to adult life in the family, at school and in society. The authors have been selected for their wide experience and close professional involvement in their particular fields. All have written penetrating and practical books readily accessible to non-specialists.

Changing
Special Education
Now

Wilfred K. Brennan

Open University Press
Milton Keynes · Philadelphia

Open University Press
A division of
Open University Educational Enterprises Limited
12 Cofferidge Close
Stony Stratford
Milton Keynes MK11 1BY, England
and
242 Cherry Street
Philadelphia, PA 19106, USA

First published 1982

Reprinted 1985, 1986
This edition first published 1987

Copyright © 1982, 1987 Open University Press

British Library Cataloguing in Publication Data

Brennan, W.K.
  Changing special education now. —2nd ed.
  —(Children with special needs).
  1. Exceptional children — Education —
  Great Britain
  I. Title II. Brennan, W.K. Changing
  special education III. Series
  371.9'0941   LC3986.G7

  ISBN 0–335–10278–6
  ISBN 0–335–10277–8 Pbk

Library of Congress Cataloging-in-Publication Data
Brennan, W. K. (Wilfred Kayran)
  Changing special education now.

  (Children with special needs)
  Bibliography: p.
  Includes index.
  1. Handicapped children — Education — Great Britain.
  2. Mainstreaming in education — Great Britain. I. Title.
  II. Series: Children with special needs series.
  LC4036.G6B74 1987   371.9   87–5780

  ISBN 0–335–10278–6
  ISBN 0–335–10277–8 (pbk.)

Printed in Great Britain at the University Printing House, Oxford

Contents

Editors' Introduction
to the First Edition

Wilfred Brennan's title, *Changing Special Education*, is both ambitious and challenging in its deliberate ambiguity. It triggers in our minds questions such as, 'How is special education changing?', 'How *should* we change it?' and 'How *can* we change it?' Few people are better fitted to examine and to answer those questions than Wilfred Brennan. Over a long and distinguished career he has both experienced and been an instrument of change; he has pioneered progress and planned and charted future developments. After teaching in day and residential special schools, and being head of the remedial deparment in a secondary school, he was a tutor at the Cambridge Institute of Education to the advanced diploma course for experienced teachers of 'children with learning difficulties'—a decade before that term was adopted by the Warnock Report. He was Inspector and then Assistant Education Officer for Special Education in the Inner London Education Authority; and, as the Director of the Schools Council project on the curriculum of the slow learner, and as a writer and lecturer, he is known to teachers in special education throughout the country and abroad. He headed a project on the application to the ILEA of the recommendations of the Warnock Report, and was awarded the OBE for his services to special education.

The Warnock Report is rightly regarded as a blueprint for progress in special education and as an immediate contribution to changing attitudes. With over 200 recommendations it is both comprehensive and far-reaching. And already, with its shift of emphasis from the handicaps to the needs of children and young people it has changed both attitudes and legislation. But blueprints and changes of attitude and emphasis alone do not meet present needs. Blueprints must be translated into laws; legislation and attitudes must become actions provisions and resources. There is a great gulf between, on the one hand, the Warnock Report's priorities and, on the other, the provisions of the new Education Act. Wilfred Brennan shows us that gulf and the steps that must be taken if it is to be bridged.

Making better provision for handicapped children and young people, and for their parents and families, is part and parcel of making a better society; that is a collective responsibility in the best interests of us all. It is the purpose of this series to explore that subject in some detail. We are grateful to Wilfred Brennan, as the author of the first book in our series, *Children with Special Needs*, for setting out so clearly the problems that must be tackled, the choices before us and the decisions we must make. It is an important and exciting look at the task of translating ideas into reality. At once authoritative and down to earth, it is a handbook for action. Administrative and organizational problems are faced as squarely as controversial issues such as integration or mainstreaming and the roles of special schools. For parents, teachers, social workers and the members of voluntary and support agencies as much as for administrators, members of multi-disciplinary teams or governing bodies and everyone interested in making a better future for those with special educational needs, Wilfred Brennan has written a practical guide. He has written with clarity and insight born of experience and deep concern. As a result he communicates both the salient features of the route we must travel and the enthusiasm and conviction we must have if we are to arrive.

Philip Williams
Peter Young

Editors' Introduction to the Second Edition, Changing Special Education Now

In this comprehensively revised edition, Wilfred Brennan has examined the impact of legislation upon administration and upon schools, the pupils and their parents. In particular he takes a penetrating look at the gap between the good intentions of the Warnock Report and the various ways in which local education authorities implement the requirements of the 1981 Education Act. For all his visionary pioneering, Wilf Brennan has always had a strong streak of pragmatism in his make-up. It is this emphasis on the critical evaluation of the practical outcomes which makes this book so important both for our understanding of what is happening today in the education of children with special needs and of what still has to be done. As he writes, there is no simple way of bridging this gap, whether it be between theorists and practitioners, resources and requirements, administrators and teachers, specialists and pupils, or between authorities and parents. Legislation alone will not achieve change. What is needed is greater sensitivity to others, recognition of rights *and* responsibilities, and 'the ability and willingness to develop a synthesis from apparently opposed positions'. If our hopes and aspirations are to become reality then this penetrating examination of 'where we are now' must be essential reading.

Philip Williams
Peter Young

Preface to the Second Edition

Some of the established practices in the first edition of this book have been relegated to historical development by the passage of time while others there looked forward to are now the current practice. As such they are treated in a more positive manner in this second edition, for they are now open to examination and evaluation as a result of which they form the basis for interim assessment of the implementation of the Education Act 1981.

The material upon which this edition is based has been gathered from many areas and I am indebted to my colleagues for their information, advice and comments freely given. They are too many to be named (and many would prefer not to be) but I here express my thanks and make clear that the implications drawn from the material remain my sole responsibility. It should also be made clear that the implications are in the nature of general impressions, though I have attempted to make them as objective and honest as possible. If they are not, that too is my responsibility.

I also acknowledge with gratitude assistance from a number of organisations, among them the NCSE, NARE, NUT, NAS/UWT, Advisory Centre for Education, the Spastics Society (CSIE), Manpower Services Commission (TVEI), MESU Special Education Section, DES (Special Education Branch) and project officers in the London Institute of Education, University of Manchester and NFER. They, of course, have no responsibility for what I have written.

Beyond the above I owe a special debt of thanks to Alan Giles, Eric Atkinson, Bob Sadler, Roy Cooper, Michael Flynn and Mike Gordon.

CHAPTER 1

What are Special Educational Needs?

All Children are Special

Every human being is an individual and each individual is unique. Even identical twins cannot occupy the same position in space and from the beginning they each perceive their world slightly different-ly. In addition, other people do not interact with or react to them in exactly the same way. As a consequence of this each twin has a different experience. This affects their perception, so that in growing to adulthood they develop their own personalities, shape their own knowledge and acquire their own skills; they remain close as individuals but the quality of uniqueness persists. Should they be separated in childhood they will each be affected by the environ-ment, social and physical, in which they grow up. For most children genetic differences are added to by the same social and environmen-tal differences noted for the twins so that divergence among individuals is greater and the quality of uniqueness more marked.

But the unique individuals are not isolated or separated. Though we are each our own person there is part of us that we share with others. Hence, though perceptions are different they have aspects which are common; though the meaning of words is personal to each, the common, shared meaning allows us to use language to communicate; and though family and neighbourhood cultures differ, common elements generate a sense of wider community which to some degree extends beyond social class, national, regional and family differences.

Teachers in classrooms cannot escape from the duality of children as individuals and as members of a group. They teach in a manner which is calculated to meet the needs of most of the group, but they know that each child will react in his or her own way, that levels of interest and motivation will differ in the group, and that individuals will exhibit different learning problems as the lesson proceeds. Some of the differences that emerge will be relatively unimportant in the classroom because they do not affect learning. Others derive their importance entirely from the fact that they *do* affect learning. It is these circumstances which interfere with learning that loom large in the classroom and the same circumstances may prescribe or restrict the informal learning in home and neighbourhood which forms part of the child's total educational experience. In the widest sense it may be said that these individual differences give rise to special educational needs and it is part of the teacher's task to identify them and to plan to meet them. The degree to which teachers do this depends upon their sensitivity to children and the level of their professional competence. Nevertheless, many individual learning needs are successfully dealt with by teachers without stress and within the constraints of the classroom and the teacher's skill. Meeting needs at this level is not usually considered to be special education but is regarded as allowing for individual differences in pupils. The term *special educational needs* is reserved for more serious or multiple needs which require more than the unsupported action of the classroom teacher. It is these needs in children, wide and varied as they are, which we will now examine.

Special Educational Needs

Special educational needs do not exist in the abstract, though it is dangerously easy to discuss them in that manner. A special educational need *always* involves a child or a young person and the immediate family as well as, in some circumstances, relatives, friends, neighbours and the professional workers involved in meeting the needs of the child in school and in the family. It is very important to keep this in mind, particularly in a discussion such as this which must inevitably rest on classification, and the generalization it entails. It may assist, therefore, to start by considering some children with special educational needs.

Barry

At 13, Barry is a good looking, freckle-faced boy with blond hair and a thin angular body. At first he appears a normal teenager. But he talks a lot and one realizes that the flow is difficult to stop. And his body never stops moving. Limbs assume a continuous sequence of new postures and the eyes are equally mobile, rarely fixing on the listener. In his flow of conversation factual reality is constantly shifted in a disturbingly egocentric manner, or subjects are changed through associations almost devoid of discernible logic. Conversing with him is demanding for the adult in a manner exceeded only by the exhaustion of attempting to keep him to one subject. In fact, Barry is grossly retarded in attainment though within normal limits of intellectual ability. His hyperactivity has proved uncontainable in an ordinary classroom and his mere presence constitutes an obstacle to learning for other pupils through the disturbance he generates and his excessive demand (or need) for the attention of the teacher.

In a small, special class, carefully structured and controlled by an experienced teacher, Barry is beginning to progress in learning and shows some signs of bringing his behaviour under control. But it is difficult to imagine how he will accommodate to any of the work situations open to him on leaving school.

Molly

Conversation with Molly is as exhausting as with Barry, but for quite different reasons. She is small and slightly built for her 11 years with dark hair and deep brown eyes. But the eyes are usually downcast and when she looks at you it is with eyes upturned from a head inclined forward. She offers no word on her own initiative and even appears not to hear what is said to her. When she does respond it is usually with one word, little above a whisper as though the sound of her own voice might shatter the stillness of her personality. Molly's level of learning in reading and number is satisfactory and compatible with her intellectual level as tested, though doubts have been expressed about the result which may well have been influenced by her unforthcomingness. But there is no doubt about the inadequacy of her social learning and her failure to respond to other people in normal situations, while her reticence makes it extremely difficult to assess her actual language competence. Molly has a depressed mother and a physical, overbearing father who, it is suspected, subjected the child to illtreatment in her early years. Social workers are concerned about the family situation but it is proving difficult to do anything positive about it.

To rehabilitate Molly successfully will require social services intervention and some changes in family relationships, but the school has an equally important task. The main task is to make Molly aware of other people, to assist her to become more positive about herself and to increase her self-confidence. Weekly sessions of psychotherapy at the local child guidance centre contribute to the task, supported by special emphasis in drama, art, music and movement in the school curriculum. At the same time all Molly's teachers are aware of the need to be positive in their relationships with her, supporting her developing confidence and encouraging her interaction with other pupils.

Jane

Jane is in a special school for children with emotional and behaviour problems. To see her in school one wonders why, unless one witnesses an episode. The violence of these is extreme. For practically no reason at all the normal 9-year-old explodes. No one and nothing near is safe and the physical violence and destruction are matched by the obscenity of language and gesture which punctuates the destruction. Physical restraint is necessary. The violence passes to be replaced by physical exhaustion which gradually gives way to a quiet reticence until, in a day or so, Jane becomes her usual apparently normal self — until the next outburst. The disruption in learning caused by this pattern is evidenced in Jane's backwardness as well as in her difficulty in keeping friends.

Expert teachers, psychotherapy and psychiatric supervision combine to assist and support the child but her 'rehabilitation' will be a long process and her education difficult.

John

John is 17 and attends a specially-designed unit for pupils with physical disabilities in a comprehensive school. Bright and cheerful, with a good word for all his teachers and school friends, he is universally liked and has responded well to the teaching offered in his school, achieving six O levels and hoping for two A levels. John's day is spent in a wheelchair for he is without legs and as his hands are appendages to rudimentary arms, he requires constant attendance to move from class to class or even around the classroom. There is no doubt about the boy's high intellectual ability which is clearly reflected in his conversation as well as by tests and by his achievements. John is a splendid example of what may be achieved by special education wherever it is given.

Robert

Robert is in a special school for pupils with physical disabilities. At first his handicap seems mild compared with John's for his body is well proportioned and normal for his 12 years. When he moves there is some slight lack of coordination and his 'reach to grasp' is somewhat haphazard; yet these are mild conditions hardly justifying his presence in a special school. It is in school work that Robert's handicap becomes obvious. His handwriting is ill-formed, irregular, unevenly spaced and practically unreadable; his reading is equally retarded, hesitant, with words missed and frequent regressions along lines notwithstanding his word-by-word attack on the print; and his apparent inability to align features on a page proves a major obstacle in his number work. Manual skills exhibit a similar lack of precision and a complete inability to work to fine limits at the level achieved by Robert's age-mates. Yet in conversation, apart from a slight slurring of words, Robert appears more at the level of his age in both interests and ability though with occasional illogical association of subjects and some misunderstanding due to lapses of attention. The latter are usually due to easy distraction by any sensory stimuli impinging on the situation, a feature noted by teachers in Robert's classroom behaviour.

Altogether, the picture is typical of many physically handicapped children. The mild physical disability has little effect on learning but serious learning problems arise from associated disabilities in the nervous system which affect perception, attention and fine motor control. The difficulties faced by pupils like Robert are easily underestimated.

Kathleen

Kathleen is lying on the floor of her classroom supported by soft cushions, surrounded by suspended 'mobiles' amid music which it is doubtful if she can hear. Without the cushions her body would have flopped like a rag doll, resting where it lay until some other person or force moved it. She has no speech and it is thought she can hear nothing but the loudest shout. Dressing and feeding are beyond her and only possible through loving, caring parents at home assisted by equally caring staff at her special school. So far as is known, Kathleen is severely mentally handicapped with central nervous system impairment resulting in almost complete physical dependence on other people; though she has little sensory perception, the teacher and welfare workers who care for her claim that there is some communication in the slight changes of expression which flit across her face from time to time. Her parents support this view and say she shows awareness when other members of the family enter a room. But to a stranger this communication does not exist.

Here is a girl of 18 years at a total dependancy level near that of a new-born infant. Kathleen shares the 'special care' which her school offers with six other children and young people with similar, severe levels of diability.

Bertie

This young man is in the same school as Kathleen but in the ordinary classes. He is a happy, talkative 14-year-old, stubby and overweight, with a shock of blond hair and the wide face, slanting eyes and protruding tongue of a child with Down's syndrome, often referred to as 'mongolism'. A closer look reveals the flattened skull, short, broad hands and roughened skin often associated with these children. Bertie is mentally handicapped but not at the extremely severe level of Kathleen. He reads a few common words, counts with a degree of accuracy to about ten and knows the common coins and their approximate value. He feeds and dresses himself in an acceptable manner, though more slowly than a normal boy of his age. Bertie's language is at about the normal seven-year-old level though he uses some words which are above that level and to other words he gives a unique, personal meaning which might be found among others in his school. Within a situation with which he is familiar, this young man behaves with considerable confidence and assurance.

Bertie has been brought to his present level through patient and careful teaching. He had to be taught many things which most children learn for themselves, so his curriculum and teaching made great demands on the staff of his school. Learning had to be presented in small steps which he could master, each carefully designed to keep him motivated, and each small success requiring immediate reward and continual repetition and reinforcement.

Anne

Anne is blind. Educationally that does not mean that she has no sight, but that she must be educated by methods which do not make use of sight. She does, in fact, perceive a shadow world and her school makes maximum use of this in training her to find her way around the environment. Otherwise use is made of her other senses to compensate for her lack of visual perception. She reads and writes braille through a series of raised dots representing an alphabet discerned through her finger tips. Anne has potentially normal learning ability and is expected to progress to normal levels of secondary education though the goals will be achieved later than by her non-handicapped peers.

Not all the blind children in her special school will make the same progress for some have intellectual and other limitations which would handicap their learning even if they had sight. Some children with very poor sight can nevertheless use it in learning and would be educated as partially-sighted children. However, it is often difficult to decide whether to educate these children as blind or partially sighted.

Donald

Donald has grave difficulty in hearing and what he does hear is so distorted that it is next to useless as a means of communication.

Indeed, it is doubtful if his hearing could meet the elementary task of offering him some safeguard against approaching danger. Hearing aids do not help him. They tend to magnify the distortions and elevate what he may just hear to a level that is uncomfortable or even unbearable. Donald is 4 and is learning to 'talk'. The specially-trained teacher in his special school takes inifinite care over the task, making sure that Donald closely observes her face, lips and tongue, touches them, feels their movement, and becomes aware of her breath on his face with attention to its pattern and force. The little boy attempts to replicate his teacher's formulation of a word. He observes her face and feels it; then does the same using a mirror to see his own. To a normally hearing person the patience required by teacher and pupil is painful and the same word could be applied to progress, for after many years the pupil's speech may mean little except to those in close contact with him. Opinion and practice differ among teachers of deaf children about how much use should be made of signing systems (sign language) and, if used, which system should be employed.

It is difficult to say where Donald's educational future will be. He is believed to be well above average in intellectual ability so he will, therefore, almost certainly learn to use lip reading as means of communication and, if his hearing allows it, his teachers will make use of highly sophisticated electronic aids to establish the inter-communication upon which education depends. Donald could achieve the goals of normal secondary education. If he does it will be through the support of expert and dedicated specialist teachers of deaf children—right from the start.

Not all the pupils in Donald's school have his level of ability and there will be those who, if they were not deaf, might require education as backward pupils and others who may be maladjusted. There are some children who through the use of hearing aids can be educated as partially hearing pupils in ordinary schools, supported by a unit for the partially hearing.

David

David is in the top bracket of intellectual ability with an Intelligence Quotient consistently around the 140 mark. He is alert, knowledge-able beyond his 13 years, a regular viewer of Open University TV programes about which he can converse with intelligence and insight, especially in scientific matters. He has wide-ranging hobbies including rock and butterfly collecting, tropical fish, gardening and greenhouse management. Yet he finds it difficult to maintain a place in the middle of a second-year class at second intellectual level in his comprehensive school. His trouble is that though he understands the tasks set and knows how to complete them correctly, he just cannot put his work on paper in the time allowed in class and his spelling is atrocious. Homework tasks follow the same pattern. A half-hour exercise for a normal pupil becomes two hours of grind for David, with all the frustration that this entails for a boy who knows exactly what is required. The finished work, though grossly immature in presentation, is equally sophisticated in content—but there is always a backlog of work devouring time.

David is receiving remedial education to counter his perceptual and fine motor difficulties even though little is known about them. Otherwise, he is being educated normally.

George

George belongs to a group of children forming the most extensive kind of educational disability. He is not mentally handicapped but his intellectual ability is such that he has great difficulty in coping with normal school learning, especially in reading, writing and arithmetic. He comes from a home which meets most of his emotional needs but falls short in the model of language that it presents to him and fails to provide the intellectual stimulation and broad experience necessary if pupils are to make maximum use of the education offered in school. Consequently George needs to learn in school many things which teachers usually take for granted and, equally, the school must provide experience and associated language which is required as a basis for George's education. This boy belongs to the wide group of pupils for long referred to as *educationally subnormal* officially, or as backward, retarded or slow learners in the shorthand of the school. Fortunately George is a stable adolescent and maintains good relationships with his teachers and his peers.

If he is to become and adult adequately meeting the personal, social and economic demands made on him, he needs an appropriate curriculum, well taught, in a situation which allows the close individual attention from the teacher that he requires for success. George is now regarded as having 'moderate learning difficulties' and pupils like him are to be found in most special schools and in many ordinary schools.

Susan

Susan has long-standing health problems. She has a mild, congenital heart condition and a long history of chest infections which have involved frequent absence from school.

When in school Susan learns normally but is retarded because her education has been subject to much interruption. It was thought that the stress of her ordinary school was a factor in her frequent infections and that a quieter, more supportive regime would be beneficial to her education as well as to her physical condition. This proved correct. Infection and associated absence have been reduced since she entered her special school and if the improvement continues she may be able to enter a special class when she enters secondary school in two years' time with, perhaps, later placement in the ordinary classes of the school.

Clarissa

Clarissa was educated in primary school and selective grammar school; she is now progressing well on her first degree course at university. Within her limitations she lives the life of any university student. And there are limitations, for she has no arms and her hands are almost at her shoulder. It would be good to think that the system in her LEA provided for Clarissa's needs, but that is not the case. Determination by her parents, initiative by a local remedial adviser, cooperation of industry in providing equipment, and the dedication of her teachers put Clarissa where she is today. Others in a similar situation may not have been so fortunate.

Most of the children described above may have spent time in hospital or may, for various reasons, have had to remain at home rather than attend any school. Hospital schools and visiting teachers (usually designated as the Home Tuition Service) provided for the children's needs in these circumstances. The descriptions illustrate the variety of conditions which give rise to special educational needs though they by no means include all those faced by teachers in special and ordinary schools. But they do reinforce the point that there is always a child or young person involved whenever there is a special need.

Disability and Handicap

There is no clear, agreed definition of the differences between terms such as handicap, disability, incapacity and disadvantage—a circumstance which introduces uncertainty in many discussions. This situation is not assisted by the fact that, whatever the term used, the individual considered is unlikely to be affected by it over the whole range of his behaviour. It has already been noted that not all the differences which emerge in classrooms affect the education of the pupils and the same is true of significant differences to which the term disability might be applied. In the descriptions of handicapped children, for instance, only Kathleen is handicapped in a manner which may affect all her behaviour; John has serious physical disabilities which will certainly affect his participation in sport and restrict his employment possibilities, but his educational achievement would be considered highly satisfactory even in the absence of his physical disabilities; and David, though unable to realize his intellectual potential in school, is involved in rich and extensive intellectual and practical activities where his disability in writing is no handicap. George has a disability which will be a handicap to learning all through school and the probability is that his educational attainments on leaving school will be restricted even if he is taught appropriately and efficiently. But when he leaves school he will leave behind the greater part of his handicap, for boys like George merge easily into the level of economic and social activities which are typical of large sections of the workers in our industrialized society. Susan presents another interesting circumstance. Her disability certainly appeared as a handicap in her ordinary school where she failed to make progress, yet in her special school the handicap was reduced and is likely to disappear in time. Throughout this change the inner condition which generated the disability remained unchanged but the change in external circumstances reduced the associated handicap. Donald and Anne both have serious disabilities which reduce to a minimum the operation of major sensory contact with the environment, and little can be done to alter this circumstance. Handicap here is almost total so far as the affected senses are concerned, though there may be some compensation though intact sensory channels. How far the disability becomes a handicap for Donald and Anne may depend on the level and patterns of their aspirations and the degree to which these require the functions of hearing for Donald or sight for Anne. For Barry, Molly and Jane the effect of their disabilities on formal school learning may be of less account than the effect on their relationships with other people. The outside world will not adjust to these children as their schools have done. Unless they achieve a degree of stability before young adulthood the tensions they will generate for others will constitute a real handicap in the workplace, in social situations and in intimate personal relationships.

From the above discussion *disability* may be regarded as a loss of capacity or function due to physical, sensory, neurological, intellectual or emotional impairment. The cause of the disability may often be determined (though not necessarily rectified) and it may also be possible to measure or assess the degree of impairment in relation to what is considered to be normal. Whether or not the disability constitutes a *handicap* is more difficult to determine and hazardous to predict for it depends on many variables. Certain disabilities handicap individuals in some situations but not in others, or for a specific period during the individuals's life. Many scholastic handicaps have this pattern. Family aspirations may create a handicap if there is insistence that the child should endeavour to succeed in an area where his disability is an obstacle to progress. The pupil's own aspirations may have a similar effect where physical disability is allied to a desire for sporting success or intellectual limitation to scholastic achievement. Disability also relates to career goals. Railway drivers and guards need normal colour vision but this may not be important for the booking office clerk; jobs requiring physical strength, stamina or accuracy of movement may be unsuitable for persons with a physical disability, or even for some persons with ill-health, but there are many jobs which do not require these attributes where their disability does not constitute a handicap. An important part of the education of children with disabilities consists of helping them to come to terms with their disabilities in the sense that they are able to shape their goals and aspirations towards areas where the disability is not a handicap and so obtain that measure of success which each individual needs for healthy living.

Age, Development and Special Needs

As children grow older they usually become bigger, heavier, stronger, understand and use more words, generate more complex sentences, become more competent socially and (most of them) better socially adjusted as self-regulation is established. It is easily overlooked that this also occurs for children with disabilities. The individual child's disability may remain unaltered but the child grows, develops and *changes*. Consequently the effect of a disability may change, in particular the degree to which it constitutes a handicap for the child. Put another way, it must not be overlooked that, even if special needs are permanent, those needs will change as the individual grows and develops. In some sad cases, such as the children with muscular dystrophies, there may be progressive degeneration of the disability leading to an increase in handicap so far as physical activity is concerned, though intellectual development may be unimpaired. For other children planned medical or surgical intervention may change the disabling condition, reduce impairment and consequently reduce or eliminate handicap in ways which may have significant consequences for their education and life prospects.

Apart from the changes in the individual child, situations may be altered through changes in the environment. Improved quality of social service support for child and family may open new prospects for education. Developments to allow the education of handicapped children in ordinary schools, or improved staffing and facilities in special schools, may lead to revision of educational plans. The introduction of new industries into a locality may open new career opportunities and these may be enhanced by an extension of the provision for pupils with disabilities to become students in Colleges of Further Education. But these circumstances, too, may operate in reverse. Lowering of economic activity may reduce employment prospects for the handicapped more than for normal workers. Cuts in social services or education may reduce the quality of care and education and inequitable allocation or mismanagement in local government may have the same effect.

It follows that any initial assessment of special needs is not of itself sufficient. It must be supported by a regular and consistent review of the disabilities of individual children and their careful evaluation in terms of changing environmental circumstances and the life prospects of the child.

Categories of Handicapped Pupils

The last decade of the nineteenth century saw the beginning of recognition and provision for pupils with marked disabilities in the growing public educational system. The growth of provision has been documented by Pritchard (1963) and summarized in Chapter 2 of the *Warnock Report* (Department of Education and Science 1978) but each extension was marked by a concentration on the *categorization* of the handicapping conditions to be provided for. Though necessary for legal definitions, the approach has had an unfortunate effect in encouraging the categorization of educational thinking. Thus, prior to 1944, Local Education Authorities (LEAs) had a duty to provide special education for blind, deaf, physically defective, epileptic and mentally defective children. The Education Act 1944 extended the duties of LEAs to securing provision, in special schools or otherwise, for children suffering from a disability of mind or body. The Secretary of State for Education was required to make regulations defining the *categories* of pupils in need of *special educational treatment* so that, welcome though the extension was, it continued the emphasis on categories and added the concept of *treatment* which put special education into a disease framework more suited to the practice of medicine than the process of education.

The outcome was a list of ten categories of handicapped pupils: blind, partially sighted, deaf, partially hearing, delicate, educationally subnormal, epileptic, maladjusted, physically hand-icapped and pupils with speech defects as defined in Handicapped Pupils and Special Schools Regulations 1959, as amended 1962, reproduced in Appendix 1. In addition the Education (Handicapped Children) Act 1970 made LEAs responsible for the education of severely mentally handicapped children previously considered unsuitable for education in school and they were included as a sub-category: educationally subnormal (severe). In the same year the Chronically Sick and Disabled Persons Act (1970) required LEAs to make arrangements for the education of children who were both blind and deaf, for those suffering from autism and other forms of childhood psychosis, and for children with acute dyslexia.

However, change was abroad and the additional categories were not brought into the close legal definitions of the Regulations. Possibly this was because of mounting criticism of the rigidity of the regulations and a growing belief that they were an obstacle to the development of special education, culminating in the broader concept of special educational needs to be discussed in Chapter 4. But there had been other changes. Over the years the pattern of defined categories of handicap changed as the virtual disappearance of tuberculosis and poliomyelitis reduced the number of physically handicapped and delicate pupils and the number of blind children also declined, though there was an increase in the number of educationally subnormal and maladjusted pupils. The number with spina bifida, a crippling condition, rose for a time then levelled off. But most marked over the years has been the increase in the incidence of children suffering from multiple handicaps which present great problems in assessment and even greater problems for the teachers who must educate the children. The rigidity of the legal definitions and the special schools organized in accordance with them made it exceptionally difficult to make proper provision for multiply handicapped children and directed attention to the limitations of a system so organized. This is not to say that the categories served no purpose, for they did direct attention to the handicapped children and provided impetus to the development of special education. But as the system developed, as knowledge and experience increased, the inherent limitations of the system became more and more obvious. And the system of special education was growing. At ten-year intervals the total number of handicapped pupils in special schools increased as follows: 1945—38,499; 1955—58,034; 1965—70,334; 1975—122,268 (DES 1979).

The population of special schools continued to increase until 1977 when there were 135,261 pupils in the schools. From that point there was a steady decline to 123,514 pupils in 1983 with the consequences shown in Table 1.1.[1]

Table 1.1   *Special school pupils in 1977 and 1983*

Category	1977	1983	Change (%)
Blind	1,255	996	− 2.6
Partially sighted	2,205	1,674	−24.0
Deaf	3,627	2,723	−24.9
Partially hearing	2,111	1,212	−42.6
Physically handicapped	13,083	11,132	−14.9
Delicate	4,404	3,249	−26.2
Maladjusted	13,687	13,395	− 2.1
Educationally subnormal			
Moderate	55,698	54,776	− 1.6
Severe	22,839	24,463	+ 7.1
Epileptic	2,096	1,447	−31.0
Speech defect	4,715	2,032	−56.9
Autistic	562	547	− 2.7
Hospital schools	8,979	5,868	−34.6
Totals	135,261	123,514	− 8.7

Note: It is highly likely that the increase in the educationally subnormal (severe) figure is the result of a policy of keeping such children in the community and returning them from hospitals rather than any overall increase in the incidence of the disability.

The overall 8.7 per cent reduction in the special school figures should be set against a 16.8 per cent fall in the total school population over the same period; actually, as a percentage of that population, the special schools show a slight increase from 1.3 per cent in 1977 to 1.5 per cent in 1983. In 1977, 16.4 per cent of the special school population were in residential special schools while in 1983 the percentage had fallen to 13.9 per cent, representing an overall fall of 22.4 per cent on the 1977 figures.

Other changes during the above period were in sex and age distributions. In sex distribution there was a slight movement towards males (1977 figures in brackets) boys, 63 per cent (61); girls 37 per cent (39). Age distribution remained fairly stable during compulsory school years but showed a slight increase for pre-school years and a significant increase in the post-school range as shown in Table 1.2.

Table 1.2   *Special schools: age distribution, 1977 and 1983 (percent)*

Year	Under 5	5–11	12—16	Over 16
1977	3.0	45.4	50.1	1.4
1983	3.7	42.9	50.0	3.3

The question is sometimes raised of the effect of special educational provision in ordinary schools on the special school numbers. For the period examined the answer must be very little, for between 1977 and 1983 the proportion of pupils receiving special education in ordinary schools remained constant at around 0.19 per cent, though the numbers (full-time) fell from 18,911 to 15,378. These figures may be considered as a proportion of all pupils receiving special education, where they represent a slight fall from 12.3 per cent in 1977 to 11.1 per cent in 1983. On the other hand, there are some reservations. Table 1.1 shows large percentage falls for the categories of partial hearing, epileptic and speech defect—all representing conditions that may easily be provided for in ordinary schools. Where that happens there may be a tendency to make placements without the formality of ascertainment procedures and this could influence the data on both special and ordinary schools.

Two other questions are of interest in relation to the period under review. How did declining numbers affect pupil–teacher ratios? And what was the effect on pupils waiting for admission to special schools? Table 1.3 sets out the pupil–teacher situation. To put them in perspective, the figures in Table 1.3 should be related to the situation in mainstream schools where, over the same period, the teaching force fell by 11.7 per cent though the pupil–teacher ratio improved from 20.2 to 18.9. In rounded terms, special school pupil–teacher ratios show a 15 per cent improvement; those of mainstream schools only 7 per cent. So far as pupils waiting for admission was concerned, Table 1.4 indicates considerable improvement. The 2,521 reduction in pupils waiting for special school places represents a fall of 37.5 per cent between 1977 and 1983, probably the result of falling rolls creating opportunities for placements. Yet much remained to

Table 1.3 Special school: teachers and pupil–teacher ratios

Year	Teachers	Change (%)	Pupil–teacher ratio
1977	16,287		8.7
1983	16,890	+3.7	7.4

Table 1.4 Pupils waiting for special school places, 1977 and 1983

	Ascertained Pupils	Pupils Waiting Places	(%)
1977	141,977	6,716	4.7
1983	126,690	4,195	3.3

be done, for of the pupils waiting in 1983 one in every five had been waiting over a year for special school placement.

Over the era of categories of handicapped pupils, then, the changing pattern is one of steady expansion in categories and numbers of pupils from 1945 to 1977 followed by equally steady decline to 1983, with the proportion of handicapped pupils in ordinary schools remaining relatively steady. The changes generally reflect the movement of the total school population. But during the decline, special school numbers held up rather better than those in ordinary schools, probably as a result of the increase in educationally subnormal (severe) pupils and the small reductions for maladjusted, educationally subnormal (moderate) and autistic pupils and the flow of pupils from waiting lists as places became available. This availability of places also contributed to the decline in the number of pupils in residential special schools, assisted by a strengthening desire to keep handicapped pupils in their own homes and communities. Against a general decline in the number of teachers employed there was a small increase in those employed in special schools, where pupil–teacher ratios improved significantly better than those in ordinary schools.

Special Educational Needs

The Education Act 1981 came into effect on 1 April 1983 and gave effect to some of the recommendations of the Warnock Report (DES 1978). Details of the Act are examined throughout the book, here it is sufficient to note the following points. First, categories of handicapped pupils were replaced by a single description of *pupils with special educational needs* with emphasis on meeting those needs through appropriate curriculum, teaching and support. Second, LEAs were required to discover and assess the children with special needs and (where considered necessary) make and maintain a *statement of special educational needs* that also specified what was to be done to meet the needs.

Consistent with these changes, from the operation of the Act onward, data on special educational provision are based upon the number of pupils for whom LEAs have made and are maintaining a statement. Strictly, therefore, post-1983 data are not directly comparable with those that have gone before, though differences in overall special school population figures should be minimal. The main difference is in the way the figures are analysed. Categories of handicap no longer appear and they are replaced by an analysis of *curriculum need* based on guidelines from the Department of Education and Science. The post-1983 curriculum categories are as follows:

Mainstream plus support A curriculum comparable with that of ordinary schools in the range of experiences it aims to cover, the skills, concepts and values it aims to develop, and the standards which it enables pupils to achieve, while providing appropriate support to meet a range of individual special needs. The support may be of such a distinctive nature, involving specially skilled teaching, that it may sometimes more appropriately be provided in particular forms of organization. It may also be in the form of additional resources, e.g. aids and ancillary help.

Modified A curriculum similar to that provided in ordinary schools which, while not restricted in its expectations, has objectives more appropriate to children whose special educational needs would not be properly met by a mainstream curriculum. Children requiring such a curriculum may be described as having moderate learning difficulties.

Developmental A curriculum covering sharply focused educational, social and other experiences with precisely defined objectives and designed to encourage a measure of personal autonomy. Children needing such a curriculum may be described as having severe learning difficulties.

In Table 1.5 the special school populations for 1984 and 1985 are analysed using the above curriculum categories with changes shown for day, boarding and hospital schools. The figures in Table 1.5 show the general downward trend in the special school population continuing, with the difference that the reduction of 3.3 per cent is now greater than the reduction in the total school population which stood at 1.9 per cent for the period 1984–5. However, as a percentage of the total school population, the special school figures show little change, down from 1.51 per cent in 1984 to 1.48 per cent in 1985. Such a small change does not suggest that there has been any significant alteration of policy on special school placement and this is confirmed by comparison with the figures for 1977 and 1983 of 1.3 per cent and 1.5 per cent respectively.

The percentage of pupils with special needs in boarding schools has shown a slight recovery: after falling from 16.4 per cent to 13.9

Table 1.5   Special school pupils by curriculum need, 1984 and 1985

| | Mainstream plus support | | | Modified | | | Developmental | | | |
	Day	Boarding	Hospital	Day	Boarding	Hospital	Day	Boarding	Hospital	Total
1984	9,929	5,956	659	58,105	7,614	462	30,212	2,930	2,339	118,206
1985	9,410	5,704	507	55,463	7,930	451	30,300	2,723	1,856	114,344
Change (%)	−5.2	−4.2	−23.1	−4.5	+4.2	−2.4	+0.3	−7.1	−20.6	−3.3

per cent between 1977 and 1983 it now stands at 14.3 per cent. Against the falling population the number of teachers in special schools remained relatively stable, showing a reduction of only 29 as a consequence of which pupil–teacher ratios improved slightly from 7.1 in 1984 to 6.9 in 1985.

Data in Table 1.5 may be converted into percentages to assess the relative demand over the three curriculum categories. This has been done in Table 1.6. Over a period of one year significant changes in

Table 1.6   *Percentage of special school pupils by curriculum need*

	Mainstream plus support	Modified	Developmental
1984	14.0	56.0	30.0
1985	13.7	55.8	30.5

curriculum are not to be expected and such proves to be the situation. What is established, however, is a firm base from which any subsequent movement may be assessed and, within that, a clear indication of where the weight of curriculum needs is to be found in special schools. The dominance of the modified level is clear and this, together with the developmental level, accounts for some 86 per cent of curriculum needs. There are, of course, some limitations to the categories of curriculum need as a basis for analysis and these may become apparent as the new approach develops.

In sex and age distribution the special school pupils remain fairly constant. Sex distribution remains the same as in 1983, with 63 per cent boys and 37 per cent girls. Age is shown in Table 1.7, where there is a welcome continued increase in the percentage of pupils at pre- and post-school ages.

Table 1.7   *Age distribution of special school pupils (percent)*

Year	Under 5	5–11	11—16	Over 16
1984	3.8	41.2	51.2	3.9
1985	3.9	40.0	51.7	4.4

The continuing decline in the special school pupil numbers should be creating opportunities for the placement of pupils from waiting lists. Is this happening, and if so what is the current situation? Table 1.8 sets out the data. The reduction of waiting lists in 1985 over 1984 amounts to 823 pupils, representing an improve-

Table 1.8   Pupils waiting for special school places, 1984 and 1985

	Ascertained Pupils	Pupils Waiting Places	(%)
1984	135,170	2,484	1.8
1985	138,210	1,661	1.2

ment of some 33 per cent on the year and to this should be added a fall from 545 to 253 in the number of pupils who had been waiting for more than one year, a fall of 53 per cent. This improvement cannot be other than welcome though there is still no justification for complacency. In fact, 253 pupils is over 15 per cent of the pupils waiting for admission or, put another way, about one in seven pupils on the waiting list for over one year. To put this in proper perspective, one need only think of what an LEA might be doing if the parent of a child allocated a special school place persistently refused to send him to school for over one year. Any argument about the damage done to the child applies equally when the LEA fails to carry out its responsibility.

To some extent the developing position in special schools cannot be fully assessed without reference to ordinary schools where a proportion of pupils with special educational needs have received their special education. An indicator of that situation is the number of pupils recorded as placed in special classes within ordinary schools. Table 1.9 brings together the data for the years 1977, 1983 and 1985. The consistent reductions in number and percentage of

Table 1.9   Pupils asertained or with statements in special classes in ordinary schools

	1977	1983	1985	Difference 1977–1985
In special classes	21,674	15,378	12,756	−8,918 (−41.1%)
% of ascertained pupils	13.80	11.70	10.00	
% of total school population	0.22	0.19	0.17	

pupils in special classes does not support the view that there has been any significant policy change about such placements in the period reviewed. However, in 1985 some 5,292 pupils with statements of special educational need were recorded as receiving education in ordinary classes of mainstream schools (figures are not available for 1977 and 1983). If the special and ordinary class figures for 1985 are combined then 18,048 pupils with statements are in ordinary schools, forming 13.6 per cent of pupils with statements and 0.23 per cent of the total school population. This situation puts the 1985 figures in a better light, but even so, the position is just about equal to that which existed in 1977, and it is difficult to conclude that there has been any significant increase in ordinary school placements between 1977 and 1985. There remains, of course, the possibility that some pupils are having their special needs met within ordinary schools without the necessity for a formal statement and (so long as it is not done merely on grounds of economy) there may be justification for this. But the consistent figures in Table 1.9 throw doubt on that possibility.

It is sometimes argued that the possibilities created by declining numbers of pupils with special needs have been offset by policies leading to the closure of special schools. No doubt there is some truth in the argument, but before leaving this review it will be useful to quantify the special school position. Table 1.10 sets out the data.

Table 1.10   Special schools and pupils in 1977, 1983 and 1985

Schools	1977	1983	1985	1985 as % of 1977
Hospital	152	115	100	65.8
Other special	1,501	1,477	1,429	95.2
All special	1,653	1,592	1,529	92.5
Pupils	135,261	123,514	114,344	84.5
Average size of schools	82	78	75	

Once more the figures reveal a relatively steep fall in the number of hospital schools. In this great significance must attach to the movement of children out of subnormality hospitals into the community and day schools, with those remaining in hospital frequently attending outside day schools. In turn, this trend must have held up the population of day schools and probably rescued some that may otherwise have been closed. Indeed the situation is more static than might have been expected given the current emphasis on provision in mainstream schools. For special schools other than hospital it could be said that 95 per cent of those open in 1977 are still open with an average reduction of only seven pupils. And, even if hospital schools are included, it appears that 92 per cent of the 1977 special schools still operate in the system. This is not to say that the closure of special schools should ever rest on numbers alone, for there are other important factors to take account of, affecting pupils, teachers, parents and curriculum.

Each Unit is a Child

The overall national situation described demonstrates the growth and extent of special education and the changes that have taken place within it. But it must not be overlooked that each unit figure represents a child, and beyond the child a family facing problems which are not experienced by the great majority of people in the community.

In the same way, each unit figure for a school or class represents a concerned group of workers, professional and others, supported by psychological, social and medical colleagues. And beyond them the clerical and administrative workers who maintain the system of special education providing the schools and resources which make it possible for those in the schools to carry out their task. Legally responsible for the whole complex are the elected members of the Local Education Authority, in particular those members who serve on the sub-committee responsible for special education. The cost of the special education is met from money raised locally through the rates and grants from the central government. But the focal point and justification for all this is the handicapped child and the purpose is to provide special education that is appropriate, efficient and compassionate.

Summary

An attempt has been made to show that all children are special in that each has the quality of uniqueness. Yet each child has something in common with others and can interact with them in a group. Teachers must take account of children as individuals and as members of a class group, the latter in the presentation of learning situations and the former through taking account of individual differences. Some differences do not affect the child's learning but those which do assume importance for the teacher. There are differences which are more than an individual teacher can cope with in the classroom and these are referred to as *special educational needs*. Thinking about needs was for long influenced by the designation of categories of handicapped children and the special schools were developed to accord with the categories. Changes in incidence of handicaps and the recognition of new handicaps put a strain on the system. But it was the increased incidence of multiply-handicapped children, difficult to place in the system, which more than anything directed attention to the inadequacy of legal definitions for educational handicap. Examples have been given of the growth of special educational provision nationally, in terms of the total number of handicapped children, and of the variety of provision through the number of pupils in each handicapped category. The beginning of the change to provision for special educational needs has been outlined together with the analysis of pupils by curriculum need, where the weight of need was seen at *modified* and *developmental* levels.

Notes

1. All tables in this chapter are derived from DES (1979; 1983; 1985a; 1985b). In the period covered, the basis for the collection of data has been changed from time to time so that, strictly, certain tables from different years are not comparable. However, any such discrepancies have been ignored as not significant to our purposes. Readers interested in explanation of the discrepancies should see Swann (1985), which also includes a close analysis of change by category of handicap.

References

Department of Education and Science (1978), *Special Educational Needs* (Warnock Report), Cmnd. 7212, HMSO.
DES (1979), *Statistics of Education (England & Wales), Vol. 1 (Schools), 1977*, HMSO.
DES (1984), *Statistics of Education (England & Wales), Vol. 1 (Schools), 1983*, HMSO.
DES (1985a), *Statistics of Education (England & Wales), Vol. 1 (Schools), 1984*, HMSO.
DES (1985b), *Statistics of Education (England & Wales), Vol. 1 (Schools), 1985)*, HMSO.
Pritchard, D. G. (1963), *Education and the Handicapped*, Routledge and Kegan Paul.
Swann, W. (1985), 'Is the Intergration of Children with Special Needs Happening?', *Oxford Review of Education*, vol. 11, no. 1.

CHAPTER 2

Discovering and assessing Special Educational Needs

The People Concerned

The discovery and assessment of special educational needs involves many people and it may be useful to list them before discussing the process itself.

Parents

Parents are the persons closest to their own child and in the natural and legal sense it is they who are responsible for the child. In normal circumstances, the intimacy of parenthood gives them access to information and insights about the child's needs which cannot be obtained from any other source. It is of the first importance, therefore, that parents are closely involved in the assessment of their child's special needs—from the start and throughout the process. Passive acquiescence is not sufficient: what is required is active cooperation to the full extent allowed by other family demands which the parents must meet. In this kind of relationship professional workers learn much from parents, but for parents also the process is a learning experience. From the experience parents gain a deeper and broader understanding of the educational aspects of their child's special needs, including the proposals eventually made for special education. More important, they are able to evaluate the proposals in a realistic manner. This desirable level of parental involvement is not always achieved, and, in particular, there is often failure to involve parents when a child in ordinary school first encounters significant learning difficulties; many subsequent difficulties may be traced back to these circumstances. Awareness of this weakness resulted in an enhancement of the parental role and its inclusion as a legal right of parents in the assessment of pupils as later sections will show.

In many instances it is anxious parents who first direct attention to the fact that their child is not making progress. They may do this through the health visitor, the family doctor or the teacher if the child is in school. Otherwise it may be a professional worker who suspects special needs and faces the problem of alerting or informing the parents. Whatever the circumstances the parents will require sensitive support which takes account of their natural anxiety, and this is more likely to be successful where parents are made aware that they are full and welcome partners in the investigation of their child's special needs as well as important participants in his or her special education.

Hospital staff

Many severe handicaps are diagnosed at birth, and the doctors and nurses involved must make the decision as to when and how the parents are to be told. If the condition is not obvious to the mother they may delay until they have consulted the family doctor and in some circumstances it may fall to him to inform the parents. Where there is doubt a medical consultant with a relevant background may see the child, and his advice may determine when and how the parents should be informed. These decisions are not easy. A natural first question from a mother is 'Is she all right'? and the answer requires sensitivity if she is not and diplomacy also where there is doubt. In the cases where there is obvious disability at birth the process of counselling and supporting the mother must begin in hospital. Fathers too must be involved and at an early stage, for the child is born into the family.

Family doctor

Whether or not the family doctor has been involved in the hospital he will certainly come into the situation when mother returns home with a handicapped child. Often he will have to deal with parents who are both upset and insecure, anxious for information, needing support and reassurance. Where signs of possible disability emerge in the first weeks or months of life the family doctor will be in a position similar to that of the hospital staff described above. He may have to refer the child to a consultant and take the decision about how the parents are to be informed.

Health visitor

The health visitor is employed by the local health district. She is a qualified nurse trained and experienced in work with infants and young children; she will make statutory visits to all mothers with new-born infants, extend the visits as required, and become the link between the mother, the local health services and clinics and the family doctor. It may, indeed, be the health visitor who first becomes aware of the possibility of special needs in the child, and to her may fall the major task of support for the mother. Where there is a long period of investigation the mother may have a special need for support from the health visitor.

Social worker

The social worker is employed by the social services department of the local council. Hers is not a medical service but she will be able to offer further support to the mother. Most often she will have been called in through the health visitor if not already supporting the family. Through the social worker the family may receive practical support, income where necessary, alterations to the house to accommodate the child's needs, contact with other parents of similar children, and an introduction to voluntary associations concerned with the families of handicapped children. The involvement of the social worker and her department will continue as long as it is necessary for the family; but the service is voluntary and it will be regulated also by the willingness of the parents to accept it.

Voluntary societies

Voluntary societies usually concern themselves with one type or range of handicap and their concern may extend from birth to the end of life. Some, such as those working with blind or deaf children, employ full-time social workers who are often well informed and experienced in the special needs of young children. Such workers are not usually involved in the discovery of special needs but their contributions may be especially valuable in the assessment of need. Otherwise the role of the societies is mainly a supportive one for the family and child though they are, in some circumstances, able to bring useful pressure to bear on central government, local authorities and the health services and this contributes to improvement in the quality of discovery and assessment.

Educational welfare officers

Educational welfare officers (EWOs) are employed by the local education authorities. They have a wide range of duties and are unlikely to be involved with children under 2 years of age, most of their work being with children over 5. It is with children whose special needs first attract attention in school that EWOs become involved. Their work overlaps with that of the social worker and where she is involved with a family regular consultation may be necessary to avoid duplication of function. Either the EWO or the social worker may contribute information about family background and circumstances to the assessment process and the question may need careful determination where both are involved. With most families there will be no social services involvement and the EWO will become the link with the LEA and the main contributor of social information in the assessment process.

Peripatetic pre-school teachers

The organization of peripatetic pre-school teaching varies between local education authorities and in some areas may not be provided. Where it is, it is usually confined to work with pre-school children who are deaf or blind or mentally handicapped. The teachers will have training and experience in the handicap with which they are concerned as well as experience with young children. They work on the basis of home visits and their role is to stimulate and teach the handicapped child, in the process teaching the mother so that she, too, becomes involved in the task with her own child. The teacher, because of her background, will be able to keep the mother informed about the schools and educational services available for her child. It is important that the teacher maintains good, close liaison with the health visitor and/or social worker and does not usurp their role but, rather, works through them where necessary. These specialized teachers should be involved in providing educational information when the children are assessed or reviewed and they should be called in whenever their specialized knowledge can contribute to the assessment of a child.

Educational phychologists

Educational psychologists are employed by the local education authorities. It is usual for an educational psychologist to have an honours degree in psychology followed by one year of teacher training, two years of teaching experience and one year of training in educational psychology. Using knowledge of child development and skill in testing and assessment, the psychologist prepares reports on the psychological aspects of the child's special needs which should be helpful both in assessment and in decisions about the kind of special education necessary to meet the child's needs. The psychologist may also be a source of advice for teachers and parents where children exhibit complex learning or behaviour difficulties.

Inspectors/advisers in special education

The designation as inspector or adviser differs among the LEAs which employ them. Whatever the title they are qualified teachers with substantial experience in ordinary schools as well as with handicapped children. Usually they have had advanced training in special education at the level of a university diploma or degree. Practice varies, but inspectors/advisers tend to have a remit over the range of handicaps together with specialization in certain areas of special need. Their first task is to supervise the work of teachers and the quality of education in special schools, special classes, or with handicapped pupils wherever they may be educated. As part of this work they organize the in-service training of teachers. In addition they are responsible for the specialized advice required by the LEA to maintain the standard of special education and develop it in response to local needs. It is also part of their remit to provide specialized educational advice and support for parents, who should have direct access to them. Inspectors in special education also contribute to the assessment of special needs and advise on appropriate school placements for individual children.

Assistant Education Officers for special education

In the structure of a LEA the AEO/SE is the administrator responsible for special education, answering to the Chief Education Officer of the Authority and, through him, to the committee of the Authority which supervises special education. Executive action on committee decisions, budgeting and organization of the special education services, conduct of the service in accordance with Education Acts and other government instructions, supervision of the work in the special education branch of the LEA; all these are part of the AEO/SE responsibility. In addition, he must formulate development proposals for submission to the SE committee and, in doing this, he receives professional advice from SE inspectors, educational psychologists, the school welfare service and the school medical service. The AEO/SE also has a role with parents. Any parents who are not satisfied with the education being offered to their child, and are not reassured by other advisers in the authority, may bring their case to the AEO. Groups of parents or associations concerned with the education and welfare of handicapped children may well raise their points with the LEA through the AEO/SE.

School medical officers

School medical officers (SMOs) are employed by the district health services. They are responsible for the statutory examination of pupils in schools and for advice about medical aspects of the conduct of the school. They have a general supervisory role in relation to individual children which is especially important for the medical aspects of children with special needs and for their parents. It is important to understand that in this role SMOs facilitate action on medical aspects of a child's condition, they do not directly treat the condition. Within the health service organization a SMO will have a specialist responsibility for offering medical advice relevant to the conduct and development of the special education service.

Medical consultants

Where a child's special needs involve a serious medical, orthopaedic or surgical condition there is usually a consultant involved in the treatment. The specialized advice may be exercised through the family doctor and the SMO is also aware of the advice and is helpful where it has implications for the school. In special schools, where there is often a concentration of pupils with consultant involvement, a trend has developed whereby consultants hold clinics on school premises to which parents are invited. The involvement of consultants in the assessment of seriously handicapped pre-school children has been noted previously. They also contribute to assessment or reassessment of handicapped children with whom they are concerned at any age. However, with children of school age the consultant's contribution is put into the assessment process through the medical element provided by the SMO.

Teachers

The whole process of the assessment of special needs and the placement of children with those needs in situations appropriate to their education may be regarded as directed at making sure that the teachers who must teach and educate the children are enabled to do so appropriately and efficiently. But teachers also contribute to the assessment process, in particular for children who are attending school. They do this through the school reports which form an important part in the examination of a child who is thought to have special educational needs. All teachers in the schools of LEAs are trained and qualified for their work and the greater part of the teaching force have years of experience with children. Intimate knowledge and experience of children with special needs is concentrated into about 35 per cent of the teaching force and approximately half of these will have additional training for their work. Almost all teachers of blind or deaf children have special training for their work as this is a legal requirement for work in these areas of disability. Each ordinary or special school has a headteacher to whom all teachers in the school are directly responsible, professionally. The headteacher is responsible for the conduct, organization and curriculum of the school in association with the school governors who are appointed by the LEA and usually include staff and parents. The responsibility extends to all children in the school, including those with special educational needs. In large ordinary schools direct responsibility for children with special needs may be delegated to a member of the teaching staff. Most LEAs have a policy encouraging a direct relationship between parents and teachers, which is of increased importance for parents of children with special needs. Parents should be aware of this and they have a responsibility to ensure that the schoolteachers are kept informed about the child and the child's needs. In doing this the parents should work through the headteacher of the school as this is the accepted professional procedure. The headteacher, in turn, has a responsibility to see that parents are kept informed of their child's progress in school and most headteachers will wish to foster a direct relationship between the parents and the class or subject teachers responsible for the child. It is now widely recognized that parents have an important contribution to make in the assessment of their child's needs and in his special education; good interaction between parents and teachers should facilitate this, but it also enhances the quality of the teacher's contribution to the assessment and reassessment of the child's special educational needs.

Child Guidance Clinics

A Child Guidance Clinic (a different title may be used in some areas, e.g. Family and Child Guidance Service) is the base for a team of workers concerned with children who have severe emotional difficulties, behaviour disorders or both of these combined. The team treats many children who remain in their ordinary schools, but when special education is thought to be necessary then the major input to the assessment process will come from the child guidance team. The team consists of the following members.

Psychiatrist The psychiatrist is employed by the district health authority or may be a consultant on the staff of a hospital. He is a qualified medical doctor who has taken further training in psychological medicine and is equipped to diagnose and treat mental and emotional difficulties or abnormalities. On the positive side he is able to offer advice about relations and circumstances conducive to good mental health.

Educational psychologist The background and responsibility of the educational psychologist have been described above, and the psychologist member of the team may work in the school psychological service with some of his time allocated to work in the clinic. In this role psychologists may be directly involved in the treatment of individual children or groups of children.

Psychiatric Social Worker Not all teams have psychiatric social workers, but where they exist they are a link with the family in the home and have a special concern for the mental health aspects of family relationships as they affect the child. The psychiatric social worker may or may not have additional training for this work but will certainly have acquired special skills as a result of experience. The interest of the PSW also extends to the child in school, a responsibility which may overlap with the educational psychologist and any other social worker involved with the family. Good cooperation is necessary here if support is to be effective without over-intrusion on family and school.

Remedial teacher Not all teams have such a teacher. When they have, the teacher functions as a full member of the team with special responsibility for educational aspects of treatment.

Phychotherapist Not all teams have a psychotherapist. This worker is trained in techniques of working with children and using therapeutic techniques which assist children to resolve their difficulties or bring them under more direct control. It is not usual for psychotherapists to have medical training though they usually have a psychology degree and training in therapeutic methods. As a general rule, psychotherapists work under the supervision of a psychiatrist. There is some overlap between the work of the psychotherapist and the treatment side of the psychologist's work; and in the absence of the former the latter may be more deeply involved in treatment.

It may be seen from the above descriptions that many workers have a role in the process of assessing special needs. Not all will be involved with each child and the particular combination is determined by the needs and age of the child, the family circumstances and even by the source from which attention was directed to the possible existence of special needs. Although the workers may vary, their disciplines reduce to education, psychology, social work, medicine and psychiatry; and the weight of each contribution is determined by the nature of each child's disabilities. But whatever the combination, the parents play a critical role and the next common factor is the need of each child for appropriate education and teaching. The latter factor cannot be too strongly stressed. Its acceptance by all workers in assessment should assist them to shape their contributions appropriately and ensure that the whole process has the proper focus which will contribute to efficiency and ensure that judgements are both appropriate and of good quality.

The emphasis now shifts from the individual workers to a consideration of their role in the system of assessment of special educational needs and the placement of pupils with such needs in suitable educational situations.

The Process of Assessment

The Education Act 1944, in addition to making each LEA responsible for ascertaining which children in its area required 'special educational treatment', prescribed formal procedures for discovering handicapped children and placing them in schools (Section 34). An 'authorized officer' of the LEA could serve notice in writing requiring the parent of any child over 2 years of age to submit the child for examination by a medical officer in order to obtain advice as to whether the child suffered from 'any disability of mind or body' and its nature and extent. A penalty (£10) was prescribed for any parent failing to present the child without reasonable excuse. The parent also had the right to request the LEA to arrange examination of a child; and parents had a right to be present at any examination, however initiated. The LEA was to consider the advice of the medical officer and reports from teachers 'or other persons' and *the LEA* was to decide if the child required special educational treatment. If it were so decided the LEA had two duties: to give notice to the parent of the decision; and to provide the treatment. If either the LEA or the parents required it, a certificate was to be issued stating whether the child was suffering from a disability requiring *special educational treatment* and, if so, its nature and extent. This certificate was to be signed by a *medical officer* of the LEA. Parents had a right of appeal against the LEA decision, to the Secretary of State for Education who could arrange for another medical examination of the child. If he decided to cancel the certificate the LEA must cease to provide special educational treatment for the child. The certificate was also necessary if the LEA intended to refer to the Secretary of State to secure compulsory power to provide special educational treatment against the wishes of the parents.

As the system developed the use of certification was found to be generally unnecessary as LEAs sought to proceed by agreement with parents. Other prescribed documents continued to be used in the less formal process and it was still necessary for the recommendation to the LEA to be signed by a medical officer. Educational psychologists completed the psychological section of the documents, though they were not allowed to sign them, and the section could, in fact, be completed by an approved medical officer who had completed a two-week course in mental testing.

It can be seen that the medical model which resulted in the categorization of educational disabilities was also continued in the concept of *treatment* and in the allocation to medical officers of decisions about the educational needs of children as well as in the categorization of disabilities as being of *mind or body*. However, as the system was tested by time and development, and as teachers and psychologists became more experienced and more confident, the unsuitability of the system became more obvious. Criticism mounted. And it was not silenced by the informality introduced into the system. Nor was criticism entirely negative, for there was much discussion and suggestion about what should replace the current system, culminating in the design of an alternative system and the establishment of field trials by the Department of Education and Science. The outcome was DES Circular 2/75.

Circular 2/75 (DES 1975) introduced significant changes. The DES prescribed national forms to be used for educational, medical and psychological reports together with a separate summary form recommending action by the LEA. The form was to be completed by a special educational adviser or educational psychologist who had seen the child, thus placing the recommendation in a firm educational context within an interdisciplinary process. In this process the roles of the workers described above were developed. However, experience of the system led to criticisms: the prescribed forms were considered over-complicated and lacking in flexibility; the co-operation required frequently prolonged assessment and delayed educational placement; and there was no arrangement for direct parental input. Yet there was a positive side. The 2/75 process stressed the need for early in-school assessment with parental involvement and the use by the school of the LEAs' professional advisers in an attempt to meet pupils' needs without recourse to formal assessment except where necessary.

Distinct Phases in the Assessment Process

Before describing the current system for the assessment of handicapped pupils and their educational placement, it is necessary to direct attention to differences between the pre-school years and those after the child enters the school system. The differences are considerable.

The pre-school phase

In the meaning of the Education Act 1944 a child is any person not over statutory school leaving age, which means that the LEA has a duty to discover and assess handicapped children from birth onward. The Education Act 1981 makes a distinction between children under 2 years of age and those between 2 and 5. Below the age of 2 the LEA may assess the special educational needs of pupils and provide special education only with the consent of parents or at their request. Assessment may be conducted in any manner considered appropriate by the LEA. Between 2 and 5 years the statutory procedures apply (they are discussed later) and parents have rights to consultation and appeal against any decision of the authority.

In the above pre-school age range the LEA may have no direct contact with the parents of children who are not attending nursery schools or classes and depends on parents, health authorities or social services departments for information about children who may have special needs. This was a weakness in the system that contrasted markedly with the growing realization of the importance of pre-school education, in particular for children in any way at risk. In an effort to eliminate the weakness, Section 10 of the Education Act 1981 placed a legal duty on the District Health Authority. For a child under 5 it has to:

Duty of District Health Authority.

(a) inform parents if a child has, or is thought to have, special educational needs;

(b) provide parents with the opportunity to discuss the opinion with an officer of the authority;

(c) bring the child to the attention of the Local Education Authority;

(d) inform parents of any voluntary body likely to be of assistance or provide advice.

In a circular offering guidance to local authorities, DES (1983) is emphatic about the quality of cooperation required if pre-school assessment and provision is to meet the needs of children and their families. Mother and toddler groups, opportunity groups, social services and other voluntary groups are identified as possibly having contributions to make in the pre-school years. LEAs are encouraged to continue to give priority to children with special needs in admissions to nursery schools or classes and to specify any necessary additional support required in the statement of special educational needs.

Another point to note is that many disabilities which directly affect learning are not apparent in the pre-school years. Moderate learning difficulty is often not obvious until the child fails the first formal learning tasks in school; emotional difficulty in the pre-school years is rarely diagnosed; and only the most severe ill-health would cause an infant child to be regarded as *educationally* at risk. Yet these account for more than half of the children receiving special education. In addition, these and many other disabilities may develop at later ages, even after the child is in school. Nevertheless, it is extremely important that all children with disabilities should be brought to the attention of the LEA even if the effect of the disability on learning is not assessable. The LEA will be forewarned and assisted in its planning, while it may be possible to arrange intervention which will eliminate or reduce the effect on learning of some disabilities.

District Handicap Teams, as proposed in the Court Report (DHSS 1976), are developing in many areas. Though a Health Service responsibility, their proper operation requires close cooperation with the LEA while their contribution will be mainly in the pre-school years and with severely or multiply handicapped children. They should complement rather than displace LEA educational assessments. *Community Mental Handicap Teams* will have a similar role in their area of responsibility.

The school years

The law relating to school attendance and the arrangements made by LEAs to ensure that parents comply with the law ensure that from the age of 5 most pupils are on a school register except those unfit to attend school or being educated under arrangements made by the parents which are acceptable to the LEA. The responsibility of the LEA to discover and assess children in need of special education has not changed, but now the LEA has access and control over the situation. Furthermore, children are beginning to be exposed to the formal learning tasks involved in education, and observation in this situation provides high-quality information for use in the process of assessment. District Health Authorities are now more closely linked with LEAs through the school health service; the school welfare service relates the schools directly to the child's home and parents; and if social services are involved with the family the probability of contact with the school is greatly increased. As a result the probability of discovery is markedly improved and the situation is conducive to improvement in the quality of assessment. The situation is also improved by the fact that the system of assessment fits the school situation more easily than that of pre-school assessment. Against this, the 'distancing' of parents from the schools which occurs from infant school onwards creates a special problem in later assessments and a positive effort is required to ensure that the views of parents are adequately represented. Nor would it be correct to assume that the assessment system works perfectly once under the control of the LEA. Milder losses of sight and hearing still too often exist undiscovered in the schools. Pupils are too often put up for assessment long after the point at which their needs should have been obvious to their teachers; once brought to notice a child's assessment may be slow in starting or unduly prolonged in execution; and the quality of educational, social, medical or psychological information may leave something to be desired. In some LEAs good-quality assessment may be frustrated because the Authority has failed to match it with a sufficiently wide variety of educational provision or through a shortfall in the amount of provision. Also, there is still a problem in securing full integration of the medical input to assessment now that the school medical service is outside educational control; and a lesser, though none the less real, difficulty in securing full integration of social services input. These problems are often operating in cases where assessment is unduly delayed or extended.

Many of the above criticisms carry over from the pre-1983 assessments to those currently operating and not necessarily without cause. Objections to the amount of paperwork involved; unproductive time built into the system; inordinate time taken to assess and place the children; and difficulty in securing the necessary cooperation among LEA 'advisers': all these are added to long-standing criticism from those who focus on system weaknesses. Such weaknesses there may well be, but it is too easy to be despondent when faced with system failures, overlooking the more frequent successful examples where assessment and placement proceed expediently and with successful outcome. Yet delay may be critical for the children concerned and there is no justification for complacency.

The System of Assessment

The approach to the discovery and assessment of children with special education needs now operating is a continuous and logical development of the system that went before it. Its basis is in the Warnock Report (DES 1978), the Education Act 1981 and the Education (Special Educational Needs) Regulations 1983 promulgated by the Act, while the spirit of the approach is articulated in Circular 1/83 (DES 1983) as it clothes the legalities with sensitivity and concern. This is the system that we now examine, first by some leading questions.

What is to be discovered and assessed?

A short answer is special educational needs in children but that only raises the question 'What are special educational needs?' A child has a special educational need if 'he has a learning difficulty which calls for special educational provision to be made for him' (Education Act 1981, s. 1). But what is a learning difficulty? According to Section 1 of the Education Act 1981:

A child has a learning difficulty if:

Learning Difficulty.

(a)   he has a significantly greater difficulty in learning than the majority of children of his age; or

(b)   he has a disability which either prevents or hinders him from making use of educational facilities of a kind generally provided in schools, within the area of the local authority concerned, for children of his age; or

(c)   he is under the age of five years and is, or would be if special education provision were not made for him, likely to fall within (a) or (b) when over that age.

There is an exemption from this definition. Children are not to be regarded as having a learning difficulty (within the above) solely because the language (or form of language) used in teaching is different from that which is (or has been) spoken in the home (Education Act 1981, s. 1(4)). But the learning difficulty must require 'special education provision' before it becomes a 'special educational need'. So, what is special educational provision? This is defined by Section 1(3) of the Education Act 1981:

Special Educational Provision.

(a)   For a child aged two years or over: educational provision which is additional to, or otherwise different from, the educational provision made generally for children of his age in schools maintained by the LEA concerned.

(b)   For a child under two years of age: educational provision of any kind.

It is clear from the above that, for a child of 2 years of age upward, a 'special educational need' exists when a learning difficulty or other impediment to learning requires educational or other support not available within the normal facilities and resources of ordinary schools in the child's LEA. Or, put another way, when the resolution of the child's special needs requires an input from outside the school's normal resources. It is the additional input that constitutes 'special educational provision'. There may be a useful distinction here between *individual differences in learning* which are accommodated within the ongoing arrangements of the school for curriculum, teaching and support, and *special educational needs* that cannot be met within those arrangements but may be met by inputs from outside educational, psychological, medical or social resources, or the removal of the child to a situation where the necessary resources are available, that is, to special class or special school. Without this (or a similar) distinction every individual difference affecting learning would become a special educational need within the meaning of the Act. The problem is, of course, that individual schools differ in what they can successfully accommodate within their normal resources, first, because what is provided for schools differs among LEAs, and second, because schools differ in the efficiency with which they make use of their resources. That is why definitions in the Act refer to the child's age and the situation in his own LEA. This may make good sense in the legalities of an Act of Parliament but it is open to a serious educational and moral objection. It is possible that a child may be denied his right to be educated with his age-group in ordinary school, not because of the inherent nature of his learning difficulty, but essentially because of the level of resources allocated to ordinary schools by his LEA, or inefficiency in the use of resources by his school.

Who is to discover and assess special educational needs?

There is no ambiguity in the Education Act 1981; it is the duty of the LEA to discover children who may have special needs and to make an assessment of the needs. The duty is clearly defined in Section 4(1) of the Act:

Duty of LEA to Assess.

It shall be the duty of every LEA to exercise their power under this Act with a view to securing that, of the children for whom they are responsible, those with special educational needs which call for the local education authority to determine the special educational provision that should be made for them are identified by the authority.

Nor are LEAs left in any doubt as to the children for whom they are responsible. By Section 4(2), these are:

(a) All pupils in schools maintained by the LEA.
(b) All pupils placed in any other school by the LEA.
(c) Where they are brought to the attention of the LEA as having, or probably having, special educational needs:
 (i) pupils registered at schools not included in (a) or (b).
 (ii) pupils not in school and not under two years or above compulsory school age.

Where the LEA is of the opinion that a child for whom they are responsible has, or probably has, special educational needs the duty is clear: 'they shall make an assessment of his needs' (Section 5).

How does the LEA discover and assess special needs?

We have seen above that, in the pre-school years, the LEA depends upon parents or health authorities to bring to its attention children who may have special needs. From the time the child starts school, however, the LEA itself becomes the main agent and its responsibility starts in the schools. The Education Act 1981 sets out certain mandatory procedures for formal assessment which are discussed later, but it also makes the LEA and school governors responsible for ensuring that there is an awareness in schools that will focus upon the possibility of a pupil having special needs from the earliest moment when he or she begins to experience difficulties with school work appropriate to age (Section 2(5)–(6)). The advice in Circular 1/83 (DES 1983) emphasizes and expands on that responsibility. Assessment is seen as a continuous process mainly concerned with describing the child's needs and the problem of meeting them with, from the start, a close involvement of parents that is continued through out the process together with progressive involvement of supportive professionals. The model was described in the Warnock Report (DES 1978, pp. 60–1):

Assessment Within the School.

Stage 1. The headteacher mobilizes information about the child's performance together with other pertinent information and, where possible, parental involvement. Decisions are made about special arrangements for the child that are within the competence of the school; execution is planned and there are arrangements for recording and monitoring. Intermediate assessments may be made and, if necessary, arrangements modified. Parents are kept involved as far as possible.

Stage 2. The headteacher is responsible for marshalling information on the child's needs, arrangements made to meet them, the progress made, the degree of its satisfaction and outstanding problems. An advisory teacher with experience of special needs is consulted about the problems. Decisions are made on future in-school approaches and/or additional inputs from normally available special needs support service. Recording and monitoring are arranged as before and parents are involved in plans.

Stage 3. The headteacher, advised by the advisory teacher for special needs, considers that more than the general routine advisory input is required in order to meet the child's needs. This could be an appropriate point for informal reference to the school psychological service, possibly through the school psychologist. There might be a new dimension to the description of the child's needs and the identification of further additional support for the school from allocated educational psychology sources. Decisions would be required. Could the new input be made informally through existing resources? If so decision and monitoring would be as in previous stages and the responsibility remains with the school. If that is not possible authority involvement may have to be considered. Should the pupil be put forward for formal assessment and determination by the LEA of his special educational needs and provision? Whatever the decision parents should still be involved. And it should be made quite clear to them at this stage that the fact of the reference for assessment does not, of itself, imply that the child's needs cannot be met in ordinary school.

In the above process it is important that pertinent medical and social information is included in the assembled material and that, where necessary, the professional workers are involved in discussions. Equally important is the involvement of the school staff, in particular teachers who have taught the child. It can be seen that recording and monitoring are important aspects of the process and the written results of these form inputs in later assessments and evaluations. They are of sufficient importance to justify a LEA policy on them with, perhaps, a proforma as a means of keeping the record. Nor should the process be seen as strictly linear, for that could amount to unproductive time for some children. Quite often informed initial discussion will establish that a child's needs call for a later stage in the process and it may be expedient to go straight to it though, unless there is a very experienced member of the school staff with responsibility for special needs, the special needs adviser

should be consulted if such a step is contemplated. In one sense the
above process amounts to a learning experience, for teachers and for
parents—and indeed for the pupil where his or her maturity
justifies involvement. The objective should be that all have a clear
understanding of the child's needs and the provisions necessary to
meet them. Where this is established the possibility of difference or
conflict between parents and school or LEA is greatly reduced.

What happens if a child is to be assessed by the LEA?

Assessment by the LEA is formal assessment that must be carried
out in a manner prescribed by Section 5 of the Education Act 1981
and the Education (Special Educational Needs) Regulations 1983.
The actual procedures are to be discussed later, but, with the
assessment completed, the LEA must decide whether or not the
child's special educational needs should be determined by the
authority. Where the LEA decides that they should not determine
the child's special needs the parents must be so informed in writing
together with information about their right to appeal against the
decision to the Secretary of State, who may, if he thinks fit, direct
the authority to reconsider the decision (Education Act 1981, s. 5(6)–
(8)). But if the authority are of the opinion that they should determine the child's needs and the special educational provision
necessary to meet them then they are required to make a *statement of
special educational needs* (Section 7(1)).

What is a statement of special educational needs?

The Act and Regulations do not prescribe the actual form of such a
statement and no official pro forma is distributed by the DES. But
the *content* of the statement is clearly defined according to Schedule
1, Part 2(3) of the Education Act 1981 and Regulation 10 of the
Special Needs Regulations 1983.

Statement of Special Educational Needs Must:

(a) describe the child's special educational needs;
(b) specify the educational provision considered appropriate to
     meet them (facilities, staff, equipment, curriculum, etc.);
(c) indicate the type of school considered appropriate and a
     particular school where one is considered suitable (except
     where parents make arrangements with LEA agreement).
(d) if education other than in school is required, give particulars
     of provision considered to be suitable;
(e) specify any additional non-educational provision needed if
     the child is to benefit from the proposed special education,

and which, if not made available by the LEA, they are satisfied will be made available by a district health authority,
social service authority or other body. If there is to be no
such provision that must be recorded.

(f) include, fully and accurately, the representations, evidence,
advice and information taken into consideration by the LEA
in making the assessment and statement.

(g) be signed by a duly authorised officer of the LEA concerned.

The Regulations contain a suggested statement lay-out and this is
reproduced as Appendix 3. Regulation 11 also stresses that
statements should be protected from unauthorised individuals and
not disclosed without parental consent except by the LEA in the
child's interest, for research and for certain legal purposes. The
statement, including matters in (f) above (which form part of it)
must be made fully available to parents.

What must the LEA take into consideration?

Regulations define the kinds of advice that the LEAs must seek in
making assessments but at the same time leave them free to seek
any advice relevant to the child under consideration. It is also clear
that the advice must be sought in the context of the child's special
educational needs. According to Regulations 3, 4 and 8, the following must be considered when assessments are made:

LEA considers when making Assessments.

(a) Direct representations by the child's parents. If oral, then by
written summary agreed by the parents.

(b) Evidence submitted by the parents or at their request on
their behalf.

(c) Written educational, medical and psychological advice,
together with any other advice considered desirable in
particular cases in order to achieve a satisfactory statement.

(d) Information relating to the health or welfare of the child
from, or on behalf of, any district health or social service
authority.

(e) The relevance of the advice and its relationship to the child's
educational needs—current and future.

(f) The provision made necessary by the advice or additional
supportive non-educational provision necessary if the child
is to benefit from education.

It is important to understand that any advice considered by the LEA in making the statement must be copied verbatim within it and must be made available to the parents. Individuals offering advice to the LEA should be made aware of this. They must also see any statements made by parents, or summaries of verbal statements that have been agreed with them, as well as evidence submitted by other advisers (Regulation 4(4)).

Who can advise the LEA?

Educational, medical and psychological advice *must* be obtained by the LEA whenever a statement is made and there are clear requirements of those qualified to offer the advice (Regulations 4–7):

1. Educational adviser
   (a) A headteacher of a school the child has attended at some time in the preceding 18 months—providing the headteacher has *taught* the child.
   (b) Otherwise a headteacher must consult a teacher who has *taught* the child within the preceding 18 months.
   (c) If (a) or (b) cannot be obtained then advice from a person who the LEA is satisfied has experience of teaching children with special educational needs or knowledge of the differing provision which may be called for in different cases to meet those needs.
   (d) If it appears to the LEA (on medical authority or otherwise) that a child is deaf or partially hearing, or blind or otherwise visually handicapped the adviser in (a) or (b) must be qualified to teach such children as the case may be, otherwise the advice in (a) or (b) shall be given after the adviser has consulted a person qualified to teach the blind or deaf as appropriate.

2. Medical adviser
   (a) A fully qualified medical practitioner.
   (b) Designated by the District Health Authority or nominated by them for the particular child's case.

3. Psychological adviser
   (a) A person employed by the LEA as an educational psychologist.
   (b) A person engaged by the LEA as an educational psychologist in the child's case.
   (c) The psychological adviser may consult another psychologist who is believed to have relevant knowledge of the child.

It is in order for advisers to consult other persons who may have knowledge of the child concerned and they must consult any such person specified by the LEA. Where a child who already has a statement (made within three years) transfers between LEAs, then the new LEA may, with consent from the parents in writing, seek educational, medical or psychological advice from the old LEA (Regulation 12). When making an assessment, the LEA must send copies of the notice to parents to the District Health Authority and the social service department. (Regulation 3). Circular 1/83 (DES 1983) is emphatic about the importance of cooperation among local authorities as a means of securing good-quality assessments, urging that precise appointments should be made to facilitate efficiency in practice. It is expected that these arrangements will ensure that necessary information and advice is made available to the LEA, but the authority also has power to seek it out. Normally, the medical adviser will coordinate advice from the DHA—including that from hospital consultants and psychiatric advice where relevant. The social services situation is not so clear, yet for some children social workers' reports may be vital. There may be a weakness here that LEAs should be aware of and seek to eliminate, possibly by the design of a local report pro forma in cooperation with social workers. To some extent the weakness noted may also apply to the school welfare service and reports from school welfare officers. The child's relationships in home and neighbourhood are always important but especially when difficulties involve emotional stress or behaviour, when a reasonably objective view of his or her life situation becomes vital. In these circumstances the social worker's report should go directly into the advice to be considered by the LEA: it is not good enough that it should be filtered through some other report. The same point applies whenever there is a possibility that boarding school placement may form part of special education provision.

What kind of advice do LEAs require?

The whole purpose of multidisciplinary assessment is that all aspects of the child's circumstances should be considered when reaching decisions about his special educational needs. If the purpose is to be achieved, advisers should be free to report within the context of their own discipline and any limitation may reduce the value of their advice. But the process also has a specific objective—to make effective the child's special educational provision. It is clear that not all the medical, psychological or social information available on the child will be relevant to the educational objective, while workers outside education may not be entirely clear about the objective itself. These facts impose a responsibility on the LEA to create a structure which, while not unduly restricting any adviser, makes each sufficiently clear about the objective to enable them to select and present from their own knowledge of the child that which is relevant to his special education. Circular 1/83 (DES 1983, para. 23) offers guidance on this point by suggesting a common approach. The child is to be considered in view of:

(a) relevant aspects of his functioning, strengths and weaknesses, relation with environment at home and school, and relevant aspects of past history;
(b) aims to which provision for the child should be directed to facilitate educational development and independence;
(c) facilities and resources recommended to promote achievement of the aims.

A checklist is suggested from which advisers may select in shaping their own contributions and it is reproduced as Appendix 4. However, in orientating advisers to the educational objective of the assessment process, it is important that they should not lose sight of the responsibility of the LEA. It is the LEA that finally determines the special educational provision to be made for the child. Therefore 'professional advice should not be influenced by considerations of eventual school placement to be made for the child' and 'any discussions individual advisers may have with parents about the child's needs should not be such as to commit the LEA, or pre-empt their decision about the provision and placement to be made for the child' (DES 1983, para. 35). Advisers should be concerned only with the child and their professional view of his needs; advice should not be shaped either by what it is possible for the LEA to provide, or by knowledge of any inadequacy in their provision. It is the child's needs that are paramount.

The task of developing good-quality multidisciplinary advice is both complicated and difficult for the LEA. The advisers must work as a team, each concentrating on his or her professional responsibilities yet aware of the roles of others. And all must maintain productive relationships with parents if their work is to be effective. Parents must be informed fully whenever their child is to be examined and have the right to be present. Though the right does not extend to certain examinations or prolonged observation techniques, good sense suggests that advisers should seek to establish parental understanding of this for nothing could be less productive than authoritarian exclusion. Above all, advisers should be seeking to reach with parents a mutual understanding of the child's needs seen from their professional background. The more successfully this is achieved the more valuable will be the advice offered to the LEA in terms of its contribution to appropriate and effective special educational provision for the child (DES 1983, paras 32–8).

What happens if there is disagreement about advice to the LEA?

There are two main sources of disagreement about advice given to the LEA—conflicting advice within the advisory team itself, and parental disagreement about the advice or its implications as set out in the draft statement of special educational needs. As advisers should see each other's contributions during the process of assessment, it should be possible to resolve many potential differences by informal discussion during the process. Where this has not been attempted, or not resolved problems, then the LEA has a responsibility to seek a solution through formal discussion with those directly concerned or in a discussion with the full advisory team. Where differences still persist it will be for the LEA, as part of the duty to assess the child's needs, to decide on 'the weight to be given to different kinds of advice' (DES 1983, para. 39). Parental disagreements may also be resolved through informal discussion, but where that is ineffective the parents have the right to discussions with the persons who offered the advice with which they disagree, or with a person believed by the LEA to be competent to discuss the advice. The procedures for this are examined later; here it is pointed out that the LEA has a duty to arrange the discussions in a way that meets the convenience of the parents. It is also wise of the LEA to warn the advisers of this possibility when informing them that parents will see the advice they offer. The possibility amounts to another reason for advisers to orientate their advice to the educational objective of the assessment as advocated earlier. It would be most unproductive if time were taken up in resolving differences about items in advice not critical to the objective of providing the special education required by the child.

How can parents obtain advice?

There are some problems with regard to this. First, there is a fine line between advice and information, and second, some parents may, especially if in disagreement, have reservations about the objectivity of advice given by officers of the LEA. These problems can be avoided through the integrity of the authority and those persons who represent it in dealing with parents—including those in the schools. The LEA is required by the Act to inform the parents of an officer from whom they may obtain information whenever a formal assessment is proposed and the selection of this person may be of critical importance. He or she must know the circumstances of the child and family and be fully aware of the assessment process, the rights of the parents, and the broad facilities and organization of the LEA. Some parents may require help in making representations and the LEA is free here to offer the assistance from its own resources or to suggest a voluntary organization or even an individual from a statutory body (DES 1983, para. 20). Whatever the source of the assistance, the person should be capable of gaining the confidence of the parents and, where they belong to a minority group, of understanding their cultural background and possible communication problems. In some circumstances it may be necessary to communicate in the first language of the parents or work through a reliable interpreter. These points should not be overlooked where parents exercise their rights to meet and talk with persons who have offered the advice to the LEA on which a statement has been made. The exchanges, by their very nature, are certain to encompass both information and advice.

Where the LEA decides that a formal statement of special educational needs is necessary, section 7(9) of the 1981 Act requires that the parents are given the name of a person to whom they may apply for *information and advice* about their child's special educational needs. The identity of such a person is not prescribed in the Act and the LEA is free to select, though the points made above remain valid. The person notified to the parents will, it appears, have a more permanent role than those discussed earlier, taking on some of the attributes of the 'named person' from the Warnock Report, so knowledge of the education service, familiarity with the kinds of difficulties creating special educational needs, and ability and willingness to maintain good relations with the family become even more essential. At the same time some degree of objectivity must be maintained if the named person is best to serve the needs of the child and his family.

There are, of course, sources of advice for parents that are independent of both LEAs and government and of great value to parents unable to obtain satisfaction through the sources noted above. The Advisory Centre for Education (ACE), the Children's Legal Centre and the Independent Panel of Special Education Experts cover the range of special needs, while other organizations concentrate on particular kinds of needs.[1] A list of useful addresses is included in Appendix 2.

How can parents appeal against LEA decisions?

The whole purpose of assessment procedures from stage one in school onward is to discover the special educational needs of the child in close and continuous association with the parents, whose views should have equal status with those of the professionals involved in the process. Assessment is seen as a continuous process in which all parties are learning about the child's needs in order to reach an appropriate educational provision. The procedures offer ample scope for the resolution of differences and it is hoped that appeals will be infrequent and regarded as a last resort (DES 1983, para. 54). Where appeals do become necessary, parental rights are clearly safeguarded in Section 8 of the Education Act 1981.

When making a statement of special educational needs the LEA *must* inform the parents of their right to appeal against the special education provision set out in the statement; that is against educational provision, the school or other arrangements, and the non-educational provision. No time limit is set for appeals though the local authorities code of practice suggests a reasonable period of not less than fourteen days and arrangements to meet the convenience of parents. Whatever the arrangements they should be made explicit for the parents who should have clear information about procedure, place and time for hearing of the appeal.

Appeals go to a local appeals committee set up under the Education Act 1980 (DES 1980) which should include members with relevant knowledge of special education. The committee will see the full statement and any additional submissions by the parents, and may call for further evidence from advisers which must be made available to the parents. Parents should be encouraged to attend hearings of the appeal.

In reaching a decision, the committee has only two options. On one hand they may support the statement as made by the authority; on the other they may remit the statement and request the authority to reconsider it in the light of committee comments. The committee has no power to overrule the decision of the LEA. Whatever the decision it must be communicated in writing to the parents and to the authority. Where the statement is referred for consideration the LEA *must* review it and inform the parents of their final decision. In these circumstances, or where the appeals committee uphold the statement, a parent still dissatisfied has a right of appeal to the Secretary of State, which the LEA should make known and assist the parent if the appeal is to be made. The Secretary of State may confirm or modify the statement or direct the LEA to cease to maintain it. These rights of appeal apply to the first and any subsequent statement of special needs.

Can parents request an assessment?

It is open to any parent to request the LEA to make an assessment of their child's special educational needs. If no statement exists, then the authority must assess unless 'it is in their opinion unreasonable' (Education Act 1981, s. 9(1)). Where the child is subject to a statement, and an assessment has not been made in the previous six months, the authority must assess 'unless they are satisfied that an assessment would be inappropriate' (Section 9(2)). The quoted phrases are open to interpretation but general compliance with requests might be expected except in extreme circumstances, for example, where a child is obviously making excellent school progress, or where a routine reassessment was due within a short period.

Is there a difference between reviews and reassessments?

Reviews of children with statements of special educational needs are a matter of routine. They are required at least annually and should form part of continous school assessment and record-keeping. Usually they will be in-school reviews, followed by full assessment where that is shown to be necessary or desirable. A reassessment, on the other hand, would follow a significant change in the child's educational or other circumstances at any time, following annual review, or parental request where thought appropriate. Transfer between special and ordinary school, or changes in home circumstances are examples of reassessment situations and there are circumstances where the effects of surgical or medical intervention make reassessment desirable. In all circumstances of review and assessment parents must be involved and their rights safeguarded (Education Act 1981, Schedule 1 Part 2(5)–(6). There is a mandatory reassessment between the ages of 13½ and 14½ years intended as a base from which to assess preparation for adult life, vocational training or employment, etc. The reassessment must be carried out unless one has been completed since the age of 12½ years (Regulation 9 of Special Needs Regulation 1983).

What happens if assessment proves exceptionally complicated?

There are circumstances where assessing special educational needs does create problems not easily or quickly resolved. Extremely rare or complex disabilities; multiple disability where placement is not easily discerned; sensory or communication deficits that make it difficult to assess the child's reaction to the environment; emotional or behaviour problems creating barriers to communication with adults; and cultural-linguistic difficulties that mask possible learning difficulties: these are examples that complicate or delay assessment and may create similar difficulties in placement. In younger children District Handicap Teams or Mental Handicap Teams may contribute to assessment, specialist hospital units may be involved, or LEAs may have developed observation/assessment units. In other circumstances placement in an existing educational situation for prolonged observation of learning or behaviour may be required. It is important that parents should understand why a provisional placement may be necessary in the event of prolonged assessment or difficulty in placement and proper parental involvement should make this easier. Nevertheless, such placements outside ordinary schools are without a statement of special educational needs and should be made with the consent of the parents. Placement should be by the LEA and should be for a clearly stated period. In some very exceptional cases it may be necessary for the LEA to provide teaching in the home.

A special case with possible complications arises when a parent is serving in the armed forces. There is a special form for reporting to the Service Children's Education Authority but it requires parental consent.

Does the Education Act 1981 apply to all parents?

The Act applies to parents of children who have, or are thought to have, special educational needs—providing they reside in England or Wales. Parents in Scotland or Northern Ireland have similar rights and duties but are covered by separate legislation. See appendix 8.

The Process of Formal Assessment in England and Wales

1.   The LEA receives a request. If from a parent, is it reasonable or appropriate? If from a school, have the initial steps been completed and does assessment seem generally indicated? If so, proceed.
2.   LEA propses to make an assessment. A notice must be sent to parents which must, by Section 5(3) of the Education Act 1981:

Notice to Parents: Proposal to Assess.

(a)   inform of proposal to assess child;
(b)   set out procedures to be followed;
(c)   name an officer from whom further information may be obtained;
(d)   inform of rights to make representations about the proposal.
(e)   state date before which representation must be made (not less than 29 days from date of proposal).

A letter might explain the situation in appropriate informal terms, in some circumstances delivered by hand by a person able to explain it and, if possible, with some knowledge of the child. There are special circumstances with ethnic minorities and these should be given serious attention.

3. LEA considers parental observations or submissions.
4. LEA makes a decision:
    (a) not to proceed—parents informed of this and also of their right to appeal to Secretary of State; or
    (b) to make an assessment of special educational needs.
5. LEA proceeds with assessment.
    (a) Parents informed with reasons for decision.
    (b) Information passed to District Health Authority and social services department.
    (c) Arrangements made for written professional advice on child's needs. Advisers provided with copies of parental representations.
    (d) Notice to parents for any examinations arranged. According to Regulation 2 of the Special Educational Needs Regulations 1983, this must:

Notice to Parents: Examinations.

  (i)   State the purpose of the examination(s).
 (ii)   State time and place of examination(s).
(iii)   Inform parents of their right to be present.
 (iv)   Inform parents of their right to submit information to LEA.
  (v)   Name an officer from whom information may be obtained.

---

6. LEA receives professional advice, which it considers together with parental representations or evidence.
7. LEA makes decision:
    (a) not to determine child's special educational needs—parents are to be informed in writing and notified of right to appeal to Secretary of State.
    (b) to determine needs and make a statement.
8. LEA proceeds with statement. Copy of draft statement is sent to parents, signed by an officer of LEA, informing them of their rights in writing. According to Section 7 of the 1981 Act, parents may:

Draft Statement: Parent Rights.

(a) Submit views on statement within 15 days;
(b) Request meeting to discuss statement with an officer within 15 days;
(c) Within 15 days of (b), if necessary, require further meetings with the persons providing the advice in the statement.
(d) Within 15 days of (c) (where held), make further representations to the LEA.

Where suitable, a school visit might be arranged for parents.

9.   LEA receives parental representations on the draft statement and reconsiders the proposal in light of them.

10.   LEA makes a decision:
   (a) not to proceed with the statement—parents are informed in writing together with an explanation of the right to appeal to the Secretary of State.
   (b) to make a statement of special educational needs.

11.   LEA proceeds with statement—unaltered or modified. Written notice must be sent to parents with copy of statement. Section 7(9) of the 1981 Act specifies that this notice must:

Notice of Formal Statement of Special Educational Needs.

(a)   contains a copy of statement which must include all advice upon which the statement is based;

(b)   explains parent's right to appeal to local appeals committee against the special educational provision specified in the statement, including the time limit for appeal and clear information on procedures.

(c)   includes the name of a person to whom the parents may apply for information and advice about the child's special educational needs.

---

12.   LEA receives parent's decision.
   (a) Parents accept statement and provision—LEA proceeds with its duty to provide the special education specified in the statement.
   (b) Parents exercise right of appeal against the special educational provision specified in the statement.

13.   LEA arranges appeal hearing. Parents are consulted and their convenience considered in arranging time and place of the hearing. They are given full information about procedures and their right to make further representations and be present at the hearing along with a friend if they so desire. Parents should receive copies of any additional evidence submitted by the LEA or called for by the appeals committee; in turn, they should make new written evidence available in advance of the hearing. Because of the duplication of documents involved in a hearing exceptional care is required to maintain confidentiality.

14.   Appeals Committee remits decision to parents and LEA:
   (a) the statement by the LEA is confirmed; or
   (b) the LEA is required to reconsider the special educational provision in the statement in the light of the committee comments on it.

15.   LEA acts following appeal committee decision. Parents must be informed in writing of committee decision or the result of reconsideration by LEA. They must be given full information concerning their right to appeal to the Secretary of State against any proposed special educational provision, and the procedure in making such an appeal, including the address to which they should write (Education Act 1981, Section 8; Education Act 1980, Schedule 2, Part 1; LEA Code of Practice). The Secretary of State will consult the LEA after which the provision in the statement will be confirmed, or may be altered, or the LEA may be directed to cease to maintain the the statement. Whatever the decision, it becomes binding on both LEA and parent with the situation regulated by the law on school attendance.

Principles of the Assessment Process

It is clear from the above discussion that the current system of assessment departs from those which preceded it in an important respect. It used to be the case that the child had to be placed in a category of handicap *before* an educational placement could be negotiated. Now the negotiation of an appropriate special educational provision must *proceed along with* the determination of special educational need, for both must be specified in the completed statement of special educational needs. It follows, therefore, that, however the LEA may arrange it, the assessment team, in addition to persons able to identify special educational needs and their implications, must also include a person or persons aware of the range of LEA special educational provision in ordinary classes as well as in special classes and schools and, indeed, provision beyond the LEA. It does not inevitably mean separate persons, for the skills and knowledge may be combined, but in most circumstances it will be advisers concerned with special educational needs who have the widest perspective of provision. Other important principles are the following:

Principles of the Assessment Process.

(a)   Close involvement of parents.
(b)   Protection of parental legal rights.
(c)   Protection of pupils with significant needs by a statement.
(d)   Description of pupils' special educational needs.
(e)   Specification of educational provision.
(f)   Specification of non-educational support necessary.
(g)   Regular review of needs and provision.
(h)   Association of reviews with ongoing school recording.
(i)   Clear definition of LEA responsibility.
(j)   Freedom of LEA to design and develop local procedures.

Though the process described applies only to England and Wales, the principles extend to the whole of the United Kingdom. In Scotland and Northern Ireland the principles are embodied in separate legislation and procedures to accord with them. See Appendix 8.

Summary

In this chapter the people engaged in the process of assessment have been indicated as parents, hospital staff, health visitors, social workers, voluntary societies, educational welfare officers, peripatetic pre-school teachers, educational psychologists, inspectors/ advisers in special education, assistant education officers for special education (AEO/SE), medical officers, medical consultants, and teachers. Psychiatrists, psychologists, social workers and psychotherapists who form the teams in child guidance clinics are also involved with children with emotional or behaviour disorders, most of whom will be clients at the clinic. Not all workers will be involved with every child, the combination and weight of contribution depending upon the child's circumstances and needs.

The early approach to the assessment of handicapped children was consistent with a medical model, related to categorization of need and the concept of *special educational treatment*. Important differences between pre-school and school-age assessments were indicated, the LEA having responsibility but little access and no control in the pre-school phase. Developments have placed responsibility for assessment with the LEA in a multidisciplinary system with a clearly defined role for the parents of children being assessed. The assessment must describe the child's special educational needs and specify the educational provision necessary as well as non-educational support. LEAs are provided with clear objectives but are left free to develop procedures suitable for local circumstances. It is noted that details of the Education Act 1981 and procedures arising from it apply only to England and Wales. The principles however, extend to Scotland and Northern Ireland, though expressed through separate legislation.

Notes

1. Parents (or those advising parents) will find detailed help, including specimen letters to the LEA, in Newell (1985).
2. Appendix 8 identifies legislation for Scotland and Northern Ireland.

References

Department of Education and Science (1975), *The Discovery of Children Requiring Special Education and the Assessment of their Needs* (Circular 2/75, Welsh Office Circular 21/75), HMSO.

DES (1978), *Special Educational Needs* (Warnock Report), Cmnd. 7212, HMSO.

DES (1980), Education Act 1980 Schedule 2, HMSO.

DES (1983), *Assessments and Statements of Special Educational Needs* (Circular 1/83), HMSO.

Department of Health and Social Security (1976), *Fit for the Future* (Court Report), HMSO.

Newell, P. (1985), *ACE Special Education Handbook* (revised edition), available from Advisory Centre for Education, 18 Victoria Park Square, London E2 9PB.

CHAPTER 3

Education for Children with Special Needs

Legislation

Until the passing of the Education Act 1944, the education of handicapped children was governed by the Education Act 1921. Part V of that Act dealt with 'Blind, Deaf, Defective and Epileptic children', the term defective relating to physical and mental disabilities. This part of the Act was separated from those dealing with elementary schools and with higher education so that, though LEAs had a duty to provide education for blind, deaf, physically defective, epileptic and mentally defective children, that duty was seen as separate from the general education provided at elementary and higher level. For blind and deaf children education was to be given in a school 'certified by the Board of Education as suitable' and similar certification was required for any school or class set up to provide education for epileptic or defective children. The Act also defined the categories of handicapped children; for example, those

> . . . not being imbecile, and not being merely dull or backward, are defective, that is to say, . . . by reason of mental or physical defect are incapable of receiving proper benefit from instruction in the ordinary public elementary schools, but are not incapable by reason of that defect of receiving benefit from instruction in such special classes or schools as under this Part of this Act may be provided for defective children (Section 55.1(a))

Provision of special schools varied greatly throughout the country, being concentrated in the large towns and cities but nowhere adequate. As a result many pupils who would have benefited from special education were left in ordinary schools (Pritchard 1963; DES 1978).

The Education Act 1944 changed this situation. Each LEA now had a duty to provide, for all children within its area, education according to 'age, aptitude and ability' and this included what the Act termed *special educational treatment*. Plans to provide SET were to be included within the general planning of primary and secondary education while, in addition to special schools and classes, arrangements could be made to educate less seriously handicapped pupils in the ordinary classes of primary and secondary schools. As the education of handicapped children in these classes is frequently regarded as a recent idea, it is interesting to examine the words of the 1944 Act in detail. According to Section 8.2(c), LEAs were to have regard to:

the need for securing that provision is made for pupils who suffer from any disability of mind or body by providing, either in special schools *or otherwise*, special educational treatment, that is to say, educational by special methods appropriate for persons suffering from that disability.

Or, to quote Section 33.2:

The arrangements made by a local education authority for the special education of pupils . . . shall, so far as is practicable, provide for the education of pupils in whose case the disability is serious in special schools appropriate to that category, but where that is impracticable, or where the disability is not serious, the arrangements may provide for the giving of such education in *any school* maintained by a local education authority or in any school not so maintained other than one notified by the Secretary of State to the local authority to be, in his opinion, unsuitable for the purpose.

Section 33.1 made it the duty to the Secretary of State to define the categories of handicapped pupils and to make provision as to the special methods appropriate to each category. Categories were defined through the issue of a Statutory Instrument (see Appendix 1) which also set down the conditions necessary for the recognition of a special school; so far as special methods were concerned, only the maximum number of pupils to be allowed in any class appeared relevant, and the number was defined for each of the categories. Otherwise education was to be suited to the age, ability and aptitude of the pupils with particular regard to their disability of mind or body, they were to attend religious worship and have religious instruction in accordance with the wishes of parents, with neither to apply contrary to parental wishes.

Since the Act was passed, other official sources have confirmed the desirability of providing special education in ordinary schools:

For the handicapped child the normal field of opportunity should be open to the fullest extent compatible with the nature and extent of his disability. The fact that he has a mental or physical handicap does not necessarily involve his withdrawal from a normal environment but, if he has to be withdrawn at all, the withdrawal should not be further or greater than his condition demands. Handicapped children have a deep longing to achieve as much independence as possible within the normal community instead of being surrounded by an atmosphere of disability, but their handicap carries with it, especially in older children, a danger of psychological and emotional disturbance, resulting from a sense of deprivation and frustration. This can often be countered by retaining them within the normal environment, or as much of it as their condition allows, provided that within it they are treated with understanding and given the fullest opportunities (MOE 1954.)

In MOE (1956) it says:

The fact that this [special educational treatment] might be given in special schools 'or otherwise' and that, in Section 33 of the Act, it was stipulated that where a child's disability was 'not serious' the special educational treatment might be given in 'any school'—i.e. not necessarily in a special school or even in a special class—served to emphasise that physical or mental handicap existed in all degrees, from the very slight to the serious; and that special educational treatment was not a matter of segregating the seriously handicapped from their fellows but of providing in each case the special help or modifications in regime or education suited to the needs of the individual child.

In that same publication reference is made to the Ministry of Education Circular 276 issued in June 1956 which stated as Ministry policy: No handicapped pupil should be sent to a special school who can be satisfactorily educated in an ordinary school.

The Act also empowered LEAs to establish special schools in hospitals, or, where the number of children was below 25, to arrange for special education under Section 56, 'Education other than in school'. The same section allowed the LEA, in 'exceptional circumstances' to provide education for handicapped children in their homes.

It may be seen, therefore, that so far as the Act itself was concerned there was an expansion in the concept of special educational provision, increase in the flexibility accorded to LEAs in providing it, the introduction of the idea of range of severity in handicap, and associated stress on making provision at a level appropriate to the disability level of individual children. These were real improvements even though the deficit model of handicap, the concept of 'treatment' and the categorization of handicapped pupils also operated as indicated in Chapter 1.

The Education Act 1981 introduced a broader concept of special education through the definition of special educational needs, as was shown in Chapter 2, and went some way to strengthening the legislative pressure for the provision of more special education within the ordinary schools. A general duty is imposed upon LEAs to have regard to 'the need for securing that special educational provision is made for pupils who have special educational needs' (Section 2(1)). This refers to the 20 per cent of pupils seen by the Warnock Report (DES 1978) as requiring special educational provision at some time during their school career. The Act then goes on to specify the duty of the LEA to the pupils with special educational needs determined by the authority through a statement—that is the 2 per cent or so whose special needs have been judged by the LEA to be 'significant':

> Where the local education authority arrange special educational provision for a child for whom they maintain a statement under section 7 of this Act it shall be the duty of the authority, if the conditions mentioned in subsection (3) below are satisfied, to secure that he is educated in an ordinary school (Section 2(2)).

The conditions are that the authority has taken account of the views of the parents on provision and that educating the child in an ordinary school is compatible with:

(a)   his receiving the special education that he requires;
(b)   the provision of efficient education for the children with whom he will be educated; and
(c)   the efficient use of resources (Section 2(3)).

It should be noted that (a) is specific—the special education is that specified in the statement. But (b) and (c) are more open, for each requires judgement and that could lead to differences of opinion. Some critics have been very hard on (c), regarding it as an 'escape clause' for LEAs choosing to use it in that manner. However that may be, the Act requires LEAs to make and maintain arrangements for special education in their areas. Section 2(4) provides that: 'It shall be the duty of every local education authority to keep under review the arrangements made by them for special educational provisions.' To discharge this responsibility LEAs will require factual information about policy and performance in discovery, assessment, placement and efficiency of educational provision for pupils with special educational needs, not as one-off reports, but as the result of a cumulative monitoring system sensitive to change. Without such a base the exercise could become merely cosmetic.

Some aspects of the Education Act 1981 go beyond the LEA and take legislation into individual schools, pre-empting parts of the system for which, technically, the LEAs are responsible. It does this by specifying the duties of school governors or headteachers in relation to pupils with special educational needs (Section 2(5)):

> It shall be the duty of the governors, in the case of a county or voluntary school, and of the local education authority by whom the school is maintained, in the case of a maintained nursery school—
>
> (a) to use their best endeavours, in excercising their functions in relation to the school, to secure that if any registered pupil has special educational needs the special educational provision that is required for him is made;
>
> (b) to secure that, where the responsible person has been informed by the local education authority that a registered pupil has special educational needs, those needs are made known to all who are likely to teach him; and
>
> (c) to secure that teachers in the school are aware of the importance of identifying, and providing for, those registered pupils who have special educational needs.

In Section 2(6) the 'responsible person' is defined as the headteacher or an appropriate governor in a county or voluntary school and the headteacher in a nursery school, so here, too, the LEA is left with little choice. The duties, however, are wide. They appear to refer to the total sensitivity to special educational needs throughout the school, to pupils identified and provided for within the school resources, and to those pupils whose needs have been determined by the LEA and for whom a statement is being maintained. And the duties go beyond the type and organization of teaching according to Section 2(7):

> Where a child who has special educational needs is being educated in an ordinary school maintained by a local education authority it shall be the duty of those concerned with making special educational provision for that child to secure, so far as is both compatible with the objectives mentioned in paragraphs (a) to (c) of subsection (3) above and reasonably practicable, that the child engages in the activities of the school together with children who do not have special needs.

This means not only that wherever possible children with special needs should be taught in ordinary schools, but that, within those schools they should, where practicable, be taught in the ordinary classes. Where this is not practicable, and children are in special classes or units, then those concerned should ensure that they participate as widely as possible in the out-of-classroom activities of the school with children who do not have special educational needs.

What is 'practicable', of course, relates directly to resources and teaching skills, which vary between LEAs and between schools as well as being matters of opinion.

There can be no doubting the fact that, so far as legislation is concerned, the Education Act 1981 has considerably strengthened the pressure for the integration of pupils with special needs within ordinary schools. Yet it has also strengthened the position of special schools. This has been done by imposing conditions where LEAs propose to close special schools, making the decision (for the first time) subject to review and approval by the Secretary of State (Section 14). At the same time the Education (Approval of Special Schools) Regulations 1983 have revised the conditions necessary for recognition of special schools to take account of the changes brought about by the Act. The Education Act 1981 has also made it easier for LEAs to provide for special educational needs otherwise than in school. Section 3 empowers the authority to do this where it is 'satisfied that it would be inappropriate for the special education provision required for that child, or for any part of that provision, to be made in a school'. The child's parents must be consulted, but the section has eliminated the 'extraordinary circumstances' required for such provision in the Education Act 1944.

Will the 1981 Act result in significant moves towards integration? We have seen above that great differences may exist between legislation and practice. Will that happen again? It may be too soon to expect authoritative answers to the question, but at least it must be examined in later chapters.

Providing Education

Chapter 1 has outlined the continual growth in special education from 1944 to 1977 with almost the whole accounted for by the increasing number of places in special schools for handicapped pupils. From 1977 onward, against a background of decline in the total school population, and with special needs provision in ordinary schools apparently static, the decline in special school places, as a percentage, was markedly less than the percentage fall in total pupil numbers (Swann 1985; see also Booth 1981; and Hegerty and Polkington 1981). And this notwithstanding the appearance of the Warnock Report (DES 1978) and the Education Act 1981 with their emphasis on integration. Are there any special circumstances that explain the dominant place of the special school in the provision of special education?

To explain the dominance of special schools it is necessary to examine developments in the main system of education. When a main system of education is under pressure there is a common tendency to isolate problems and make separate provision for them so that the main system may continue to develop more effective methods to meet majority needs. Also, the task of developing specialized subsystems is usually easier than attempting to introduce increased variety and complexity into the main system. It is undeniable that these circumstances have operated in the development of the public system of education. In the normal course of development it might be expected that as main system problems are resolved and effectiveness improves there should be some move to incorporate the separate subsystems within the main framework. Here, too, there is evidence in education. Periods of low pressure in the main system saw the tentative development of units for partially-hearing pupils within the ordinary schools and some growth in provision for slow learners. But the truth is that the main system has rarely been free from pressure. The reorganization of secondary education in the tripartite system; the raising of the school leaving age; the move to comprehensive secondary education; the revolution in primary school methods followed by experiments in middle-school organization; the extension of the new primary methods into secondary schools; the growing demand for nursery education; the exceptional growth of further and higher education; the effect of stop-go economic policies by successive governments and the continuously erosive effects of monetary inflation have kept the main system under almost continuous pressure. In these circumstances the development of the special schools subsystem may have been an appropriate and reasonably successful response. But it carries with it a serious danger: the success of the special schools subsystem may create a belief that there is no possible alternative. This ignores its circumstantial origin and endows it with an apparent inherent validity that powerfully resists challenge or change.

This discussion is not intended as a criticism of special schools. They do have serious disadvantages, though most of these arise from the separation of the pupils from their normal fellows, and for this the teachers in the schools are not responsible. The same teachers, aware of the disadvantages of the special school, have developed methods to compensate through interaction with ordinary schools and 'linked' courses with colleges of further education. And they have, in many instances, developed the special methods of teaching which make it practicable to consider the education of some pupils with special needs within the ordinary schools. The main purpose of the discussion so far is to show that, though there was no legislative obstacle to the development of special education within ordinary schools, conditions may have prevented the development through facing those responsible for the system of education with an almost continuous series of problem pressures. For the purpose of a chapter concerned with the provision of education for children with special needs, and with their placement in situations appropriate to their education, the result is that available alternatives to special school placement are restricted. Furthermore, while special schools offer good opportunities for the placement of pupils with a clearly-defined major disability, serious difficulties arise if the disability is moderate, and needs support but not necessarily at the level of a special school. Even greater difficulty arises in placing pupils with multiple special educational needs. This is not so much because special schools are unwilling to admit such pupils but because, as the schools themselves would freely admit, there is little experience in the system in meeting with an acceptable degree of success the problems these children present. The result is that anyone concerned with the educational placement of children with special educational needs becomes well aware of the fact that the needs range widely from the mild to the severe and increasingly occur in multiple form for the same child. Logically it might be expected that arrangements for the education of children with special educational needs would follow a similar pattern. In fact they do not: and this poses a major difficulty in placement for an increasing number of children.

Placing Children with Special Needs

We have already noted that, in the current system of assessment, provision, that is the placement of the child in an appropriate situation for special education, must be considered along with the description of the child's special educational needs. This is necessary as both must be specified in the draft statement to be considered by the child's parents. Where possible an appropriate school or unit should be named, while, at least, the type of placement must be specified. The approach to the formulation of the statement and placement differs among LEAs as they respond to local circumstances or even to the circumstances of individual children. In many LEAs the weight of work falls on educational psychologists, in others on special needs advisers; some have made specific appointments of experienced individuals to collate reports and write the statements, others leave the task to the assistant education officer for special education. The individuals concerned use their judgement about communication with the 'advisers' who have written the reports that form part of the statements: they may discuss points with individuals, call meetings of groups or even the whole statement team according to the problems they identify in the reports. Other LEAs have introduced group procedures. In one approach the 'statement group' seeks to be involved as a group throughout the formulation of the statement, bringing in the 'advisers' as indicated above. In another version the group meets initially to consider submissions after which the individual statements are allocated to the person in the group with the most relevant experience or knowledge. That person then completes the draft statement as an individual task but brings it back to the group for consideration before it is finalized for the parents. Whatever the system adopted in the LEA (and many are still experimenting and seeking an ideal) an exceptionally sensitive and efficient administrative support is necessary, especially where parents exercise their right to comment on statements and meet the persons who have advised the authority.

However the statement of special educational needs is formulated, it is, in principle, a recommendation to the LEA, for it is the LEA that is legally responsible for providing special education and for placing individual children in the situation most appropriate for their special educational needs. Though much depends on the size of the LEA and upon its organization, there does seem to be an advantage in the placement decision being influenced by an inspector/adviser in special education. In their role they are likely to spend more time in special schools and classes than the educational psychologist who has much wider terms of reference; their experience of teaching handicapped pupils with special needs is usually more extensive; their training in and experience of curriculum, classroom organization and general school policy is wider than that of most psychologists; and inspectors/advisers, through their visits to schools outside the LEA, usually have a wider concept of all available possibilities than their psychologist colleagues. Nevertheless they will require good briefing from those colleagues where there are special considerations involving specific learning difficulties of individual pupils. It must be clearly realized that these comments refer to the role of the psychologist and inspector or adviser. An individual educational psychologist may have teaching experience far greater than the nominal two years required in the profession; and some inspectors/advisers in special education are educational psychologists.

The task of advising on the educational placement of a child with special educational needs involves bringing together two sets of information. The adviser concerned must know as much as possible about the individual child and his or her needs. This information comes from the statement papers described in Chapter 2. While considering these the adviser will be forming ideas about the kind of curriculum the child needs and the type of school likely to provide it. At this point the second set of information requires consideration. Of the schools appropriate, which is most suitable for this child? To answer this question the adviser needs a great deal of information about the schools. A whole stream of questions follows. Must it be a boarding school or a day school? If a day school, which is most suitable for access in terms of travel and links with the child's family? What are the differences in the curricular strengths of the schools and which most closely matches the child's main needs? Are there any special teaching strengths in any of the schools which are particularly appropriate for this child? What are the general levels of pupil behaviour and type of discipline in the schools and how do these relate to the pupil? What is the past record of the schools in meeting the needs of children similar to this one? Have there been recent changes in any school which might affect the ability or willingness of staff to meet the needs of this child? Is any school affected by change of headteacher or staff? Will it change the evaluation of the school in any way? Have the parents expressed any preferences for this or any other school? How do these schools relate to parents? Which is likely to relate best to the parents of this child? Is there one school which is clearly the most suitable for this child? Or are schools X and Y equally suitable? Should the parents be asked to visit one school and reach a decision before, if necessary, being invited to visit another? Or should they be given both schools to visit and their choice accepted? Questions like these formulate in the mind of the adviser considering the placement, and he may also labour under some frustrations: the most suitable school may not have a vacancy appropriate to the age of the child; is there a reasonable alternative or would it be better to wait for a vacancy in that school; and how long would the wait be? There may be no vacancy in a suitable school and the adviser may have to consider seeking a place outside the LEA. How would the parents view that? Would it mean boarding school? If so, is it proper to advise that the child should be educated away from home because of lack of places in the LEA? And so the questions go on.

An adviser in the above situation faces a complicated task which is made more difficult by certain features of the current situation in most LEAs. First, though the description of pupil needs is far from satisfactory, it is usually better than current techniques for describing school regimes. Second, school strengths and weaknesses usually reflect those of the teachers who form the staffs; hence staff changes often imply school changes. And though children change as they grow and develop, changes in schools are frequently much more rapid as staff arrive and leave. Third, the previous point means that a school suitable for a child when placed may lose the very strengths that had indicated the school as the most suitable choice. Fourth, however good an adviser may be, his assessment of a school has inevitable limitations. Fifth, very few LEAs have yet devised a means by which schools may keep the LEA aware of their strengths and weaknesses or the changes which affect every school. And sixth, few LEAs have a sufficient variety of special schools to allow real and meaningful choice in the placement of children with special educational needs. Furthermore, where placement with special support in an ordinary school is indicated by the child's educational needs, the choices available to the adviser making the placement are usually even more restricted than the choice of special schools. Given the situation described, it would not be an overstatement to say that ideal placements are rare and that most represent a compromise in the sense that they are the best possible and available in the current circumstances.

In view of what has been written above the efficiency of the system of special education may be questioned. Yet the fact remains that by far the great majority of placements work out well for the children and satisfy their families. How can that be? It is highly probable that the degree of success relates to the flexibility with which special schools approach the problems presented by the children placed in them. Teachers in the schools and the advisers who place children are aware that needs as at present described only very broadly indicate what the child requires. More precise definition of the pupil's needs arises during his teaching and learning in the school, and the regime is gradually accommodated to them. Add to this the natural resilience of children (often underestimated by adults) and accommodation becomes a two-way process, supported by the care and concern for children which is the outstanding feature of special schools. And these same features appear in the best work observed where children with special needs are educated within the ordinary schools. More than anything, the lower pupil–teacher ratios and the reduced pressures in special schools and classes make this possible through the intimacy which they allow between teacher and learner. But though these features contribute to success they also bring dangers. The most serious of these is the danger that the schools and classes may demand too little of the pupils in terms of their scholastic attainments. It may be that most pupils lose by this, though the main concern must be for those pupils who, though with disabilities, have the potential to follow a normal academic curriculum. In this respect those in special schools are most at risk through the small size of the schools, the limited staff numbers and the consequent restriction of the curriculum. All these considerations will be in the mind of the adviser as he contemplates the possibilities and reaches a decision about the child.

The decisions reached in the above process must appear in the specifications of Sections 3 and 4 in the statement of special educational needs which the adviser must be prepared to discuss with the child's parents should they so desire. In practice, where good relationships exist, there is much to be said for seeking parental views during the formulation of the statement, or for similar discussions with the headteachers of suitable schools, in order to extend the information base for the decision and secure agreement through participation. In exceptionally difficult cases agreement about the type of placement necessary might be followed by arranging parental visits to potentially suitable schools in order to decide placement after the statement has been agreed.

Similar procedures to the above are necessary where a handicapped pupil is to be placed in a special class within an ordinary school, especially if it involves the transfer of the pupil from a current ordinary school. In general such a placement is more easily accepted by parents and it is not usually necessary to become involved in the long discussions that often precede placement in a special school. One complication is that in some instances (especially where difficult behaviour is involved) there may be a difference of opinion about a pupil's suitability between the headteacher of the school and the teacher with responsibility for the special classes. Yet it is important that both should be involved and, if possible, agree with the admission. Another factor is that the existence of special classes often increases parental opposition to special school placement. In these circumstances parental pressure may lead to proposals for special class placement of pupils who might be better placed in a special school, with consequent objections to admission from the head of the ordinary school on the advice of the teacher in charge of special classes.

A more common difficulty arises from a lack of special education provision in ordinary schools combined with inadequate provision of special school places. In these circumstances pupils who could profit from special education in an ordinary school cannot be so placed because the support they would need is not available in the school. Placement in a special school then becomes inevitable and is deeply resented by parents who recognize the situation. At the same time, headteachers of special schools are often reluctant to admit these pupils when they have children on their waiting lists with a much greater need for what the special school can offer. However this situation is resolved, a child is denied access to appropriate special education—at least for the time being. This represents a failure of the LEA to discover the children in its area who require special educational treatment and to make arrangements to provide it: a duty placed upon LEAs 35 years ago in the 1944 Education Act. It is not surprising, therefore, that parents, teachers and advisers become frustrated and angry about such situations.

LEAs now have a duty to provide for each child with a statement the kind of education specified in the statement and in the named school where one is indicated; they must also provide the specified educational and non-educational support. The effect should be to bring more order and permanency into the arrangements for special education in ordinary schools. Where designated special classes exist in the school their facilities and curriculum should be clearly identified in the school account of internal arrangements required by the Education Act 1980.[1] When pupils with special needs are to be educated in ordinary classes their statements will specify the support to be provided. These changes should take the arrangements out of the area of negotiation between headteachers and advisers and establish a firm base from which responsibility and performance may be assessed. The clearer definition of resources for special needs should make more difficult their diversion to other purposes within the school or the abandonment of arrangements whenever the school faces a crisis. Yet the advantage carries with it a danger. The specification of resources may itself motivate a demand for statements that overrides the actual needs of the child and is seen as a way of adding to the resources of the school. There have been suggestions (as opposed to proof) that this is appearing: if so it should be vigorously resisted as a perversion of the system.

Another frustration arises where the non-educational support required is not within the control of the LEA—i.e. speech therapy or physiotherapy. The District Health Authority may be unable to make provision for many reasons, or may be unable to provide the level indicated in the statement. Few LEAs have the resources to make good those shortfalls and the situations involve much unproductive use of administrative and advisory time as well as delays that may be damaging to pupils.

There are times when advisers are faced with children for whom school placement is not a possibility but who none the less need appropriate education—for instance, children with serious disabilities in the pre-school years. If the LEA has organized a service of pre-school home teachers then the problem is simply one of including the child in the schedule of an appropriate teacher. In the absence of such a service (a not untypical situation) the adviser may have to consider an *ad hoc* arrangement with the staff of an appropriate special school or rely on the fortuitous availability of a teacher willing to visit. Exactly the same situation exists where children are unable to attend school and must be educated at home—whatever their age. A child in hospital where there is no hospital school presents the adviser with similar problems. Either a hospital school must send in a visiting teacher or a part-time teacher must be found for the task, which is complicated by the need to relate teaching to the curriculum of the school to which the child will return. For other than short-term arrangements inclusion of provision in a statement should ensure permanency for as long as is required.

It has become apparent in the discussion that advisers responsible for the school placement of children with special educational needs in situations where facilities are inadequate or restricted face a daunting task. In small LEAs it is not unusual for the special education adviser/inspector to have a whole range of other duties in ordinary schools. These include: organization of in-service training; advice to schools on internal arrangements to meet the needs of slow learners or other pupils with problems; advice on suitable books and equipment for the task, and guidance on the appointment of teachers for work in these schools. At the same time, the AEO/SE will, no doubt, be looking for advice on how to improve the inadequate service. Though the educational psychologist can share some of this task, he cannot share the professional supervision of the schools or responsibility for the quality of special education. An adviser may be in discussions with parents who are unaware of his workload and regard him as being exclusively concerned with the education and well-being of their handicapped child. Considerations of this kind have resulted in proposals by the Warnock Committee for improved advisory services.

The Range of Special Provision Required

Provision in different LEAs varies so much that to select and describe a typical situation would be misleading. It is proposed, therefore, to list the reasonable range of provision which should enable an education authority to meet most of the special educational needs in its area. The list is quoted from the Warnock Report (DES1978, p. 96)

- full-time education in an ordinary class with any necessary help and support;
- education in an ordinary class with periods of withdrawal to a special class or unit or other supporting base;
- education in a special class or unit with periods of attendance at an ordinary class and full involvement in the general community life and extra-curricular activities of the ordinary school;

- full-time education in a special class or unit with social contact with the main school;
- education in a special school, day or residential, with some shared lessons with a neighbouring ordinary school;
- full-time education in a day special school with social contact with an ordinary school;
- full-time education in a residential special school with social contact with an ordinary school;
- short-term education in hospitals or other establishments;
- long-term education in hospitals or other establishments;
- home tuition.

The list is not exhaustive. Nevertheless, consideration of it in relation to the placement difficulties outlined in this chapter shows that the range of provision, with sufficient places, would resolve most of the difficulties.

The Objective of Comprehensive Provision

Only when comprehensive provision matches the range of special educational needs will placement cease to be a matter of compromise. That is the first objective. The second is to place each individual, no matter what the kind or degree of disability, in a situation where he or she is able to interact as fully as possible with children who do not have special educational needs. Even with comprehensive provision the objective will require careful planning and a broad concept of what integration means. The Warnock Report (DES 1978) identified three essential levels:

Locational. This relates to the physical location of special classes or units in an ordinary school or the sharing of a campus by special and ordinary schools. It is a minimal form of integration which may only be suitable for exceptionally severe disabilities of great deviance. But even then it may create conditions of awareness between the groups with understanding and sensitivity for the children without special needs.

Social. The location may be as above but there is planned and extended interaction between the groups. Joint teaching programmes may not be realistic but in all other school activities children with special needs participate with other children. Interaction and communication should be established in the mixed groups.

Functional. This is the fullest form of integration. Children with special needs share as far as possible in ordinary school programmes and teaching—full-time or part-time. Social and out-of-school activities are on a mixed group basis.

The three levels both broaden and sharpen the concept of integration. Each has its own validity for some children yet all share the same objective, differing only in degree and that determined by the special needs of individuals. Yet they should not be regarded in a deterministic manner. As in all aspects of education, the possibility of development should never be abandoned. Therefore, as later discussion will show, the levels need not be thought of as requiring separate provision, for only flexible situations are equipped to offer immediate and continuous response to development in individuals. That is why integration and its potential should have specific consideration when reaching decisions about the placement of children with special educational needs. It is not enough that a school can offer the teaching and curriculum required to meet the child's special needs; it should be able to meet them in a situation that offers appropriate level of integration with the potential to extend it as the child develops. The importance of this is such that it demands thorough discussion with the child's parents, for they will have their part to play with the school. It also justifies spelling out the broad approach and objectives in the child's statement of special educational needs.

This focus upon integration could become one of the most important aspects of the Education Act 1981. Not because it can be immediately achieved as a norm of the system, but because its importance in assessment and placement brings education authorities to a realization of the absence of facilities for its achievement in many areas and their responsibility for developing them. It should also concentrate minds within the schools as realization grows of the specific responsibility for children with special needs imposed by the Act.

Another effect of the range of provision would be to create pressure for more careful and detailed descriptions of children's special education firmly within the frame of ordinary education, so that placements may be made more accurate and appropriate. Similarly, the same pressure would operate to make reassessment more positive in order to utilize the range of provision available.

Summary

This chapter has shown how the Education Act of 1944 placed special education firmly within the frame of ordinary education, made possible provision in ordinary schools, widened the scope of special educational treatment and extended the definitions of handicapped pupils. But it also showed that the opportunity to provide special education in ordinary schools was neglected and expansion confined mainly to special schools. The lack of ordinary school provision penalized most those pupils who could have followed a normal school curriculum with support. Multiply handicapped children were also difficult to place in schools developed to reflect specific categories of handicap.

A definition of 'special educational needs' replaced categories of handicap following the Education Act 1981. The Act also made it a duty of LEAs to educate children with special needs in ordinary schools whenever possible in association with children without special needs. It is suggested that, up to 1985, there had been no major movement in the direction of such integration.

The problem of placing children with special educational needs in appropriate places for education has been shown to be complex, in particular where the range of needs is not matched by the range of provision. The flexibility with which schools and children accommodate to each other appears to overcome many inadequacies in the system.

It is suggested that the Education Act 1981 should, as it is implemented, assist advisers in the tasks of placement and bring permanency to arrangements made in ordinary schools. The range of such arrangements desirable is illustrated with the suggestion that their provision would remove many current problems in the placement process. Three levels of integration are identified as necessary if integration is to have specific consideration when placing children with special educational needs. It is suggested that the levels do not imply separate provision but should form part of flexible arrangements.

Notes

1. The Education Act 1980 and the Education (School Information) Regulations 1981 require LEAs to publish information about the local education system and individual schools, including special educational needs and 'particulars of curriculum and other special arrangements' of individual schools.

References

Booth, T. (1981), 'Demystifying Integration' in W. Swann ed., *The Practice of Special Education*, Open University Press.

Department of Education and Science (1978), *Special Educational Needs* (Warnock Report), Cmnd. 7212, HMSO.

Hegerty, S. and Polkington, K. (1981), *Educating Pupils with Special Needs in the Ordinary School*, NFER.

Ministry of Education (1954), *Report of the Chief Medical Officer, 1952–3*, HMSO.

MOE (1956), *The Education of the Handicapped Pupil 1945–55*, HMSO.
Pritchard, D. G. (1963), *Education and the Handicapped*, Routledge and
    Kegan Paul.
Swann, W. (1985), 'Is the Integration of Children with Special Needs
    Happening?', *Oxford Review of Education*, vol. 11, no. 1.

CHAPTER 4

What Should be Done

What does the Education Act require of LEAs?

Each LEA must now think in terms of children with special educational needs and organize a local system that will ensure that they are discovered, their needs identified, and special education provided—wherever possible within ordinary schools and in association with children who do not have special needs. Where a child's learning difficulties, or other disabilities, are significant the LEA must afford the protection of a statement of special educational needs, review it annually and maintain it so long as it is judged to be necessary. Parents must be involved when the statement is first proposed and at all reviews and, if not in agreement, they have the right of appeal against the statement or the special educational provision within it. To assist parents the LEA must name officers who will give them any information they require and, eventually, the name of a person to whom they may apply for information and advice about their child's statement, his needs or the special education being offered or provided by the LEA. Where the young person remains on a school register the LEA is responsible for education up to the nineteenth birthday and must assess further education or employment needs when the child is between 13½ and 14½ years of age. The LEA has a specific responsibility to ensure that the 'responsible person' is identified in each school and performs in the schools the duties imposed by the Act in maintaining awareness of children with special needs and their education as well as the identification of emerging special needs among children in the school. It is obvious, therfore, that the LEA has full responsibility for special education in its area and that includes keeping the system under review so that it remains sensitive to and adequate for local needs.

Are LEAs Implementing the Act?

We shall note later work that is in hand to produce reasonably objective information about the Education Act 1981, but, in 1986, the question may only be answered through a loose collection of opinions and subjective judgements.[1] There seem to be two main bodies of opinion. The optimists are convinced that the Act will eventually accomplish something positive because it directs attention to problems, allocates responsibility, and seeks to change attitudes in a manner calculated to motivate action in the direction of change. They see the focus of that change as the extension of provision for children with special needs within ordinary schools in the manner set out in the Act. Pessimists focus on the real or imagined shortcomings of the act. They point to the way implementation depends on resources—and the manifest failure to inject any additional resources into the system of special education. Lack of resources, they argue, is reinforced by what they call 'escape clauses' in the Act that refer decisions to local opinions of 'practicality' or 'efficient use of resources' within the framework of prevailing conditions. If ordinary schools do not have the resources to resolve the problems already in them, how can they be expected to provide for pupils with even more demanding needs? they ask. Others point to the high degree of cooperation required between local statutory bodies that, individually, are hard pressed to meet their own social and legal obligations. Above all, pessimists point out the importance of teacher-training implied in implementation of the Act and show how lack of resources has limited effort in that area. It is possible that these bodies of opinion reflect the experience of the individuals within them. Certainly if one took an overall view the impression created would lead to pessimism: but if one looks at the examples of good practice (some to be described later) then they support an optimistic view of what could be achieved.

But if there is a lack of information there is no shortage of anxiety and concern. General teachers' associations, associations concerned with special education, and parents associations are collecting information on implementation.[2] Four research projects supported by the DES will report on implementation, support for ordinary schools, and teacher's courses—we describe these in more detail in Appendix 5. In the near future there will be better-quality information, but meanwhile we present the outcomes of our own less structured enquiries based upon discussions with and reports from colleagues in special education in different parts of the country. Among concerns about the implementation of the Education Act 1981 are:

Negative Features of Implimentation.

(a) inconsistency in provision among LEAs;
(b) descriptions of needs are overinfluenced by available provision;
(c) variation in policy on statements between LEAs;
(d) tendency in some areas for statements automatically to lead to special school placement;
(e) inadequate support for pupils with statements placed in ordinary schools;
(f) widely varying policies in relation to parent information and involvement;
(g) lack of policy on and records of in-school assessment by LEA;
(h) absence of clear LEA policy often with fortuitous nature of some very good examples of school pratice;
(i) difficulties in collating and integrating advice from health and social services when making assessments;
(j) uncertainties about provision of non-educational support when providing bodies lack resources;
(k) length of time required to make assessments.

In a more positive frame some situations have been indicative of what may be achieved throughout the system given more experience and some small increase in resources:

Positive Features of Implimentation

(a) Local policies based upon consultation between elected members, officers, teachers, parents and community organizations.
(b) Healthy and positive attitudes to integration in LEA and schools.
(c) Well-planned LEA guidelines for ordinary schools.
(d) Good organization of school coordinators for special needs.
(e) Well-planned 'awareness' courses for teachers in ordinary schools.
(f) Willingness to experiment with new roles for special schools.
(g) Conversion of 'remedial services' into support services for special needs.

Throughout our enquiries it became obvious that certain general difficulties facing almost all LEAs were to some extent outside their control. First among these is the general lack of resources followed closely by, and possibly associated with, the absence of a positive lead on integration from government or DES. In most urban areas schools are facing serious problems unconnected with special needs—such as those generated by falling rolls and consequent reorganization. And these are the areas where, even within existing resources, recruitment of teachers is often a major problem. The circumstances naturally generate anxieties in teachers who face additional demands in their schools. Another factor outside the control of the LEA is the level of resources and efficiency in the Health Service and during the period of the enquiry changes were afoot in the service that made rational planning more difficult than ever.[3] Overall, though, it was difficult to avoid the impression that the authorities doing well were those that had achieved good-quality services before the 1981 Act came into operation. Perhaps this is not surprising: after all, there are few principles in the Act that were not objectives sought after by many LEAs in the years before 1981.

One final point that came across during our enquiries should be set against the data in Chapter 1 that indicate little progress towards integration. Many people made reference to the lead-time in planning and finance that operates in local authorities.[4] They believed that there were projects in hand only just on the point of reaching fruition. The optimists were convinced that, as a result, an acceleration of activity could be expected in the near future with implementation gaining in pace and breadth. One hopes that this is a realistic expectation and that the above attributes are matched by depth and quality.

A Broader Concept of Special Education

The broader concept of special education is in direct contrast to the categories of handicapped children which operated before the Education Act of 1981. For the categories that Act substitutes the concept of *special educational needs* taken directly from the Warnock Report (DES 1978). A description of the special educational needs of the individual child becomes the objective of the assessment process; while special education consists of the arrangements made to meet the described needs—wherever those arrangements may operate. In the report, special educational needs were seen as those which required special provision in the location, content, pace, timing or methods of education; broadly, physical, sensory or mental disabilities and emotional or behavioural disorder but including any other condition, or combination of conditions which create educational difficulties for a child which cannot be resolved by a teacher, unaided, in the classroom.

The Warnock Committee saw this approach as one which would bring many more children within the scope of special education and for two main reasons. First, the concept of special educational needs extends beyond consideration of specific disability and takes account of the total situation of the pupils as it affects their education. Second, in addition to pupils with permanent special educational needs, there are others who will have special needs at some point in their educational development, though the needs will not be permanent. At any one time, one in six children are likely to require special education while one in five will require it at some point during their school career. These, of course, are the planning estimates made by the Warnock Committee and experience suggests that there will be wide variation between different, individual schools.

One difficulty in attempting to operate with the broader concept of special education rests in contradications associated with the Education Act 1981. The Act is intended to provide a legal basis for the operation of the concept, but the legal phrases necessary in the Act become a barrier to the concept. This can be seen when the definitions of the 1981 Act and the Warnock Report (DES 1978) are directly compared. Let us look first at special educational needs.

Special Educational Needs.

Warnock Report.

Pupil requires: special means of access to curriculum through special equipment, facilities or resources; special teaching techniques; special or modified curriculum; modification of the physical environment; particular attention to social structure or emotional climate in which education takes place.

Education Act 1981.

Pupil has: significantly greater difficulty in learning than the majority of children of his age; a disability which prevents or hinders him from making use of educational facilities of a kind generally provided in schools, within the local authority concerned, for children of his age.

Definitions in the report are positive and concentrate on what is required to support learning and development as near to normality as is possible for the pupil. In contrast, the legal definitions of the Act are negative. They concentrate on what the pupil cannot do in a manner reminiscent of the deficit model which prevailed before the concept of special educational needs. The Act is also relative in referring definitions to the child's LEA where the subjective judgement of what is 'significantly greater' must be made. Quite apart from any inequity this may create between individuals, the operation of the definition produces no pressure to improve the quality of local provision.

Contrasts similar to the above also operate in the definitions of special education. Here, too, the Report is practical in the sense that the facilities can be identified in the schools and positive in that they relate to the definition above of special educational needs. The Act, on the other hand, retains its relativity by reference to the child's LEA and carries with it again the danger of inequity between individuals and lack of pressure for the improvement of local provision.

Special Education

Warnock Report.	Education Act 1981.
S.E. identified by: effective access on a full or part-time basis to teachers with appropriate qualifications, or substantial experience or both; effective access on a full or part-time basis to other professionals with appropriate training; an educational and physical environment with necessary aids, equipment and resources appropriate to the child's needs.	Special educational provision means: for a child who has attained the age of two, educational provision which is additional to, or otherwise different from, the educational provision made generally for children of his age in schools maintained by the local education authority concerned; in relation to any child under that age, educational provision of any kind.

It is difficult to avoid the conclusion that the Act fails to fulfil the main purpose of a central government which should be to establish a standard below which no LEA is allowed to fall but above which any may rise. It is also pertinent to ask what is to carry most importance, the prevailing local standard or the identified special educational needs of the child? So long as this ambiguity remains it is not surprising that in some circumstances descriptions of special needs appear to be unduly influenced by what the child's LEA is able to provide.

The purpose of the above discussion is to draw attention to differences between the Act and the Report that are of some consequence for the future of special education. There are two main dangers. The first is that some authorities may begin to believe that the Education Act 1981 is the implementation of the Warnock

Report and therefore lack motivation to go beyond it; the second is that the very existence of the Act may divert attention from the many recommendations in the Report that do not require an Act of Parliament for their implementation. The truth is that the Act provides a real (if limited) basis for action to implement the Report, but any LEA striving for high quality will find the pointers in the Warnock Report definitions rather than in the Education Act 1981.

The broad concept of special education should not be taken to imply that one child in five with special educational needs will be handicapped in the sense of the categories of handicap created as a result of the 1944 Education Act. Part of the broader concept is the recognition that there are many real needs in young children which affect their learning, often in a temporary manner, generate frustration from failure, reduce the benefit which should accrue from education and build up to serious obstacles to learning. Early recognition of the needs followed by appropriate action intervenes in the above cycle, rescues the child from the negative situation, and for many prevents the development of more serious problems. This should form much of the special education provided in ordinary schools and the major part of the extension of special education implied in the broader approach of the Warnock Report. It is to be regretted, therefore, that the Education Act 1981 places its main emphasis on provision for children whose special education is the subject of a statement by the LEA and consequently does not stress the importance of preventative special education within the ordinary school and the needs of the large number of children who require special provision though not at the level which merits a statement by the LEA. In a similar manner, the Act empowers the Secretary of State to make regulations governing the recognition of a school as a special school but does nothing to establish the basic facilities to be made available in ordinary schools which provide education for children who are the subject of a statement of special educational needs. These omissions in the Act will not prevent any LEA from making excellent special educational provision in its ordinary schools but they could lead to ill-conceived attempts at 'integration on the cheap' as an alternative to special schools in a period of financial stringency.

On one thing the Warnock Report and the Act agree: special schools will continue to be required for some children with special educational needs. Currently these schools are providing education for between 1 and 2 per cent of the total school population—that is about the percentage of pupils for whom statements are expected following the 1981 Act.[5] Chapter 1 indicated the relative stability of the special schools in the years since the operation of the 1981 Act and in the short and medium terms this stability may be expected to continue. But some change is inevitable. As valid and appropriate designated provision is made in ordinary schools for the special education of children with needs determined by the LEA the effect will be felt in the special schools in a manner to be discussed in Chapter 5, but it is too early to assess either the speed or extent with which the development may take place in the absence of adequate resources.

However, the long-term consequences of the operation of the broader concept of special education can be anticipated. Gradually there should be considerable extension of special education provision within the ordinary schools, mainly consisting of pupils whose needs were not previously recognized in any organized manner, but including also some children who might formerly have been placed in special schools. At the same time the recognition that special educational needs may be temporary, or may change as the child develops, requires improvement in the flexibility with which the system of special education responds to changing needs in children and young people. This will not be achieved unless there is considerable interaction between the different situations in which special education is offered: that is, between teaching in ordinary classes, in special classes organized within ordinary schools and the designated classes in those schools which are initiated by the LEA, in support groups within the school or on other premises and in the special schools. Full use of the flexible system will require improved methods for assessing and describing special educational needs and the school regimes necessary to meet them, allied to more sensitive and regular reviews of children's needs. At this point it may be useful to give further consideration to what is implied by the Warnock concept of special educational need.

In recommending the abandonment of the existing categories of handicap and their replacement by the description of the special educational needs of individual children, the Warnock Report recognized that there would still be a need for descriptive terms for groups of children with similar special needs. The existing descriptions of children with sensory or physical disability (blind, partially sighted, deaf, partially hearing, physically handicapped) are considered acceptable. Use of the term 'maladjusted' was considered acceptable within strict limits though in practice it has been replaced by 'emotional and behaviour difficulties' (EBD). But the committee regarded the term 'educationally subnormal' as imprecise, assuming agreement on what was educationally normal, and suggesting intrinsic deficiency for what are mainly social and cultural deficiencies. The term 'educationally subnormal' has been abandoned and replaced by the description 'children with learning difficulties'. To accommodate the wide range of learning difficulties a level is indicated: 'mild' to describe pupils whose needs might be met within the resources of an ordinary school; 'moderate' for those pupils with needs that require placement in a special school or a designated class in an ordinary school; and 'severe' for mentally handicapped children.

References to 'delicate' children still appear to have some currency though they may well fall into disuse in the future. Those children with illnesses which generate physical disability or require special medical attention may join the physical disability provision, or, where the effect is mainly on learning, the learning difficulties group, the precise placement being indicated through the description of their special educational needs. Similarly, where illness affects behaviour, the needs of many children may best be described by the new meaning of emotional and behaviour difficulty. It is important to note, however, that the terms are merely descriptions of children with similar needs: they are *not* categories of handicapped children, and they have no legal meaning in terms of the Education Act 1981. The decision about special education is to rest on the needs described for the child and the measures proposed to meet them and *not* upon whether or not he or she can be placed in a legally-defined category of handicap.

Planning the Development

Resources and achievement

The changes implied in the Warnock Report will require more than the broadening of the concept of special education. To achieve that objective requires the extension of special education into the pre-school years and its continuance into further and higher education, improved contributions from the supportive health and social services, and a degree of cooperation between the three services only rarely achieved at the present time. All these things make demands on expenditure. More buildings, improved equipment, additional professional and other workers, improved standards of training, and better information services for parents and the community will increase demands on central and local government budgets at a time when central government is unwilling to increase expenditure and is also applying maximum pressure on local authorities in an attempt to reduce their expenditure. In these circumstances bringing about the changes will not be an easy or short-term task. The circumstances call for careful and efficient planning of the transition to the new system, for cooperative approaches by the three services to make maximum use of scarce resources as well as the integration of voluntary effort in public planning to avoid unnecessary duplication of effort and to ensure that initiative or enterprise is fully utilized wherever its origin may be.

But even if the economic situation were easier, the transition would still require efficient and cooperative planning and it would be neither wise nor expedient to move rapidly across the whole front of special education. Some of the necessary changes have in them an inescapable time element. Education, health and social services must abandon their suspicion of each other; improved teacher training cannot be achieved overnight; and public attitudes to the disabled will take time to become more accepting and less patronizing. Within the schools themselves attitude changes are necessary if change is to be effective. Teachers in the ordinary schools need time in order to become confident that they can educate children with special needs in their schools and to realize that doing this for some children is not a 'second best' or cheaper alternative to a special school. Teachers in special schools also need time to realize these same things and to admit that some of their children might, in fact, receive a more appropriate special education in an ordinary school. Both need to lose their sense of exclusiveness as a necessary condition for easier and continuous interaction between ordinary and special schools for the benefit of children with special needs.

Teacher training

Changes in teacher education are crucial. All teachers in initial training need to be made aware of special educational needs as something they will meet in schools, should be able to recognize in a general manner in the early stages and allow for in their work. They should be aware of a teacher's potential contribution to the assessment of the pupil's needs and to meeting them where possible in the ordinary classroom. This should be backed up by a general awareness of the sources of support for classroom teachers in their work with children with special needs, and for the children directly, which is related to some knowledge of the different forms of special education. During their training the young teachers should have some contact with special schools and classes. That element of training is present in some courses; it requires urgent extension to all. LEAs can do little about the development except exert pressure on those who prepare teachers. But they do have control over the in-service education of the teachers in their schools. The Warnock Committee estimated that about three-quarters of the existing teaching force required additional courses to establish the objectives proposed for initial training. Clearly this is a task for LEA action and most now have a cadre of experienced teachers and advisers who could conduct the courses, if necessary with cooperation between adjacent LEAs. An important part of this work will be to make teachers aware of local support services and skilled in their use, while induction courses to achieve it will be necessary for experienced teachers who join an LEA and take responsibility for children with special needs. The scope of these courses should include the introduction of teachers to the local health and personal social services. Cooperation between the services to operate joint courses would add quality to the work. Some areas are of special importance to teachers working with children with special needs. Working with parents and non-teaching assistants; peripatetic teaching and work with pre-school children; and the principles of guidance and counselling are examples which should be developed beyond the level indicated above. In addition teachers working in special education should not be allowed to lose contact with developments in teaching in major curricular areas as has sometimes happened in the past and this aspect of in-service work is important. There will be a continuing need for teachers who have studied the problems presented by children in the different groups of special educational need at the level of current one-year full-time courses in special education.

There has been some progress in teacher training. Many LEAs have developed local courses mainly concerned with 'awareness' aspects and the training of school coordinators of special needs; some have developed work based upon precision teaching using behavioural methods, while others have concentrated on the production of teaching materials using video-recordings covering child development, learning and classroom practice. There are examples of these in Appendix 6. The DES was early in the field with a tape-slide presentation covering 'awareness' while in-service training of teachers for children with special needs in ordinary schools (SENIOS) has had an injection of funds as a priority area. Micro-electronics in special education has had similar allocations at about £3 million, much of it for equipment and teacher training.[6] The Advisory Committee on the Supply and Education of Teachers reported on the special needs element in initial teacher training with suggestions for changes and the need for such training was accepted in the White Paper *Better Schools* (DES 1985). The Committee also reported on the scope and relevance of existing in-service courses. It is in the latter area that there is currently some unease. There are proposals to end the pooling arrangements upon which the advanced one-year courses have been developed and to make grants for training dependent on local authority-specific proposals to the DES where eventual control will reside. The DES is known to favour one-term courses which have had some success in SENIOS and are well regarded by some LEAs. The future pattern is not yet clear but there can be little loss if teachers have access to a greater variety of courses; if selection can be made more rational and related to local use of teachers returning from the courses; and if courses taken early in the teacher's career concentrate on the improvement of practical classroom teaching skills. But the need for good-quality advanced one-year courses will remain for the system needs the input of intelligent, academically sound and research-influenced practitioners as headteachers, advisers and teacher-trainers equipped to take the system forward and maintain and improve its quality. Perhaps the best one-year university courses should be maintained for this purpose with more rigorous selection of entrants, based on classroom competence and performance on the shorter courses. If this is to happen then some permanent financing arrangements will be necessary, both for the teachers concerned and the providers of the courses (Mittler 1986; Holt 1981; DES 1985b).

Local cooperation

The broader concept of special education will extend the area of cooperation between education, health and personal social services at local level. Special education will no longer be almost exclusively provided in special schools so some of the necessary contributions from the other partners will be required at more input points—for instance to the ordinary schools and the designated classes in them. The probability is that a greater proportion of the input will be from the local community services rather than school-based services as developed in special schools, so the pattern as well as the extent of services will change. The extension of special education to the pre-school years will create a special problem of cooperation in the intimacy of the family at this level. The post-school extension will create a different problem, for the young person concerned acquires more personal responsibility at this level, particularly in medical matters. But the responsibility is not always recongized by parents of handicapped young people a fact which can create real problems for supporting professionals. It will be necessary to recognise much more clearly than in the past that the role of the services changes as the baby becomes child, then a schoolchild, an adolescent and a young adult. At each stage the service to take the lead should be defined according to the needs of the client. These problems will also appear at district and regional level where the client has complex needs or resources are scarce. Thinking and planning to identify the problems and explore solutions should start at once on a cooperative basis.

A basis for cooperative planning already exists in the Joint Consultative Committees set up in the revision of the National Health Service in 1973. The committees are formed from elected members of the Health Authority and the Local Authority to advise the constituent authorities on matters of common concern where the interests overlap. Some strengthening of the JCCs will be necessary if special educational provision for children and young people is to be brought within their operation. One suggestion is that there should be a working party of officers concerned with children and young people with special educational needs to keep provision under continual review. Such a working party would require membership from special education, social services, health and the careers and employment services at senior officer level. This suggestion of the Warnock Committee merits examination and exploration, but there are difficulties. The working party could easily become large and unwieldy as it would have to coordinate work with regional organizations in special and further education and with Manpower Services.

Special education regions

Special education has a regional organization which is based on nine groupings of LEAs. At present they form a forum for discussion of common problems, discuss regional planning taking account of the voluntary bodies and undertake a limited amount of regional in-service work in special education. If there is to be more positive regional planning aimed at regional self-sufficiency their work will require strengthening. Links with the Joint Consultative Committees are desirable and the Warnock Committee suggested that the membership should be extended to representatives of health and social services, to elected members as well as officers and to teacher representatives. The planning of special education in further and higher education will require cooperation with regional and national bodies responsible for planning those areas of education. These moves, if brought about, will require extremely careful organization. Some regional conferences in special education will become exceptionally large, the administrative load from their work will correspondingly increase and their work may well change in a qualitative manner. There is a danger that the regional conferences may fall into the hands of professional administrators, or that the educational element may be swamped by the additions from other services. It will be necessary to guard against this, for to carry out its task appropriately the regional conference must remain an *educa-*

tional forum. It is possible that new proposals for in-service training could involve the regional organizations. The LEAs involved could use the region to cooperate with universities and polytechnics in developing local patterns of courses to meet regional needs common to all the members.

Planning problems

There are many more mundane but equally important problems to engage the attention of special educators in the LEAs. A planning base must be established upon some estimate of the size of special education likely to develop in ordinary schools. At its lowest level this will require space in the schools properly located in terms of the input required from health and social services. To provide space requires consideration of population trends related to a review of school buildings. And for many sensory disabilities (such as blindness and deafness) a nice balance is required between what may be provided locally on a day school or unit basis and what will be required on a residential basis involving cooperation between adjacent LEAs, or regional planning which may include the voluntary bodies. The outcome of the exercise will influence plans in many ways. The number of teachers required in special education, the levels of their training and responsibility, the number of non-teaching assistants, child-care workers and domestic staff, the workloads to be postulated to health and social services as a basis for planning their input to the schools: all these will rest on careful estimates and projections in the special educational section of the LEA. They will be the direct responsibility of the assistant education officer for special education and he in turn will rely on sound educational advice from special education advisers or inspectors.

Advisory and Support Service in Special Education

The concept of an advisory and support service (A&SS) in special education arises directly out of the recommendations of the Warnock Committee and is based upon what the members observed during their work. No doubt in the form described it is an elaboration of existing good practice in a number of LEAs. In this section it is proposed first to describe such a service, and subsequently to consider why it is necessary.

First let us examine the duties of an A&SS. These may conveniently be sectionalized as work with ordinary schools, work with special schools, advice to the LEA, and advice and support for the parents of children with special educational needs.

In ordinary schools

The first responsibility of the A&SS in ordinary schools is to raise the quality and extend the scope of special education in them. This responsibility is shared with the headteachers of the schools and requires that the advisers work closely with the teachers in the classrooms. There will be a need for direct teaching of some children by the staff of the A&SS, not only to meet the needs of the child, but as an effective way of ensuring that the skills of the advisory teacher are transferred to the class teacher. To support this the A&SS has a responsibility for the organization of in-service courses for teachers in the schools and for ensuring that they have access to and make use of appropriate teaching aids and materials. Arrangements for the assessment of children with special needs must be known in the schools and headteachers will require advice on appropriate levels for individual children; they should look to the A&SS for both of these. Most important, teachers taking up work with children with special needs will need local induction courses.

In special schools

Here, too, the A&SS shares with headteachers the responsibility for the quality of special education in the schools. Advisory teachers will probably have less need to work directly with children in these schools though their advice will be required in relation to some children with complex or multiple disabilities, in which role they will bring to the school the specialized knowledge of members of the A&SS. A very important part of A&SS work will be to foster interaction between special schools and other situations where special education is provided; to make sure that special school teachers do not lose contact with wider developments in teaching; and to ensure that special schools do not become isolated in the system as they have tended to do in the past. There will be a need for A&SS contributions to higher-level and specialized courses for teachers in special schools which will require cooperation with other A&SS and call for knowledge of the work of very specialized special schools operating on a regional basis.

In the LEA

The A&SS is the source of professional advice on the quality of special education in the LEA, assessment of its efficiency in meeting the range of needs encountered and promulgation of proposals for development. In this role the A&SS works through the assistant education officer for special education. The advisers will also be concerned about the in-school assessment of special educational needs and the provisions made to meet them, keeping the AEO/SE informed about them and making sure that the administration is aware of any inadequacies. Where children with complex or multiple needs must be placed outside the LEA advice about placement will come from the A&SS which will also be responsible for reporting on the situation and on the progress of children so placed. The LEA will also look to the A&SS for advice on the staffing of schools, the promotion of teachers, appointment of headteachers and first appointments to the Authority wherever these involve the education of children with special needs.

With parents

The A&SS is the source of professional advice for parents about the education of their children who require special education. At pre-school level the main link will be the teachers working with children in their homes. In the school years it will mean reassuring parents about placements, school routines, outcomes of reviews or any other educational problem causing them concern which cannot be resolved by the headteacher of their child's school. There will be times when the senior adviser may become involved in complex situations where parents are at odds with the LEA. In this situation, and indeed whenever advice to parents is involved, it is important that advisers should be accorded the right to advise parents exclusively on the basis of what is best for the special education of the child, otherwise the service will be unable to obtain and hold the confidence of parents. The situation does create difficulty within an LEA, and there will be times when advisers struggle with divided loyalties, but there is a sense in which they are sometimes the defenders of the child against the LEA or even the parents. This part of the A&SS work is made more important by two interconnected circumstances: firstly, the Education Act 1981 requires LEAs to appoint a 'named person' to safeguard the rights of children for whom the LEA maintains a statement of their special educational needs. Second, the Act requires the LEA to *name* an officer of the authority from whom further information may be obtained when informing a parent of a proposal to assess a child's special educational needs. Together these factors may be expected to extend the responsibilities of the A&SS in special education.

In carrying out the above important and extensive duties the A&SS will have to interact and cooperate with other sections of the LEA, for instance, the school psychological service, the school welfare service, and other parts of the local inspectorate. In addition, at the operational level, the A&SS will be the point of contact between the LEA and the health and social services in meeting the needs of handicapped children and their families. There does appear to be a need to improve the service of LEAs to families. A survey carried out by the Spastics Society (Rogers 1986) revealed that only about half the LEAs gave clear information on parental rights; one in three failed to spell out the basic steps in assessment; only half mentioned their duty to secure the provision in the statement; and a quarter their duty to keep it under review. There was much variation in ideas about the role of the 'named person' even among LEAs drawing attention to it while none developed the idea of the named person as a 'befriender'. Within the LEA the A&SS may be well placed to take on the tasks of parent education and information in a combination of individual counselling and provision of courses, perhaps in association with the adult education section of the LEA.

Staffing the A&SS

Because of the range of local variations it is not practicable to spell out staffing levels for an A&SS, but it is possible to suggest an outline staffing structure. There is a need to have clear and unambiguous responsiblity for a service as important and complicated as the A&SS so a senior adviser is required with relevant training and experience as head of the service. He will need to work closely with the AEO/SE and the head of the school psychological service but he should be directly responsible, professionally, to the principal adviser of the LEA. The main body of the service should consist of advisory teachers with a breadth and depth of knowledge about special educational needs greater than would normally be expected on the staff of a school. To them would fall the duty of continuous advice to schools about, and where appropriate the teaching of, pupils with special needs. When necessary they would call for support from the peripatetic advisory teachers described below. The work of the advisory teachers would be almost exclusively in the ordinary schools and they should be a source of expert advice on the teaching of pupils with learning difficulties and on curriculum modification necessary to meet their needs. The organization of the work of these teachers could be based upon the grouping of a number of schools or on an area of the LEA, but however determined, it is important that the responsibility should be clear and adhered to. A continuous presence in their schools is an essential part of the work of advisory teachers if they are to gain the intimacy with children and staff which is essential for high-quality work. Groups of advisory teachers may be supervised by colleagues with senior responsibility for a team. Such team leaders, in addition to their general work, should have expertise in a specialized area of special need appropriate to the level of pupils in special schools and designated classes and to them would fall the task of bringing together teachers from ordinary and special schools. They would also organize local courses. Consistent with the broad range of special education, the A&SS would need a smaller group of peripatetic specialist teachers to be concerned with children for whom the LEA has made a statement of special educational needs and who have been placed in special schools or designated classes. They will need expert knowledge of at least one of physical disability, severe sensory loss, mental disability, emotional and behaviour problems, speech or language disability and severe specific learning disability. Within the group there should be teachers experienced and trained in the special educational needs of early childhood. These are the teachers to work with pre-school children and their parents in their homes and to contribute to assessment at that level. An important part of their task will be contact with, and advice about, playgroups, nursery schools, toy libraries and other sources of educational support for the children and their parents.

All these teachers should contribute to assessment at the appropriate levels which are discussed below. But to make their work fully effective they need special links in each primary or secondary school with a teacher who has responsibility for children with special needs and is the direct link with the A&SS.

On first reading, the above organization may seem elaborate or even over-elaborate, but it is necessary. The extensions into ordinary schools make it imperative that each headteacher should have direct access to advice about children with special educational needs. The teachers responsible for teaching the children need the confidence which comes from good communication with an insightful, experienced colleague as well as the opportunity to observe him at work. And schools will require advice about their internal assessment based upon deeper knowledge and wider experience than is likely to exist on the staffs of ordinary schools. Special schools, in future, will face problems of severe and multiple handicap and more will be expected of them. The headteachers and teachers will require advice from advisers experienced in different handicaps who can contribute to the resolution of problems presented by difficult combinations of special educational need. There is also the central problem of improving assessment, in particular its educational component, and of describing school regimes so that they may be matched to the described needs of individual pupils. An informed presence in the schools is essential if these system requirements are to be satisfied. At the same time there is a pressing need to improve the quality of special education and, in particular, to promote the development of improved curriculum in all areas of special education—including the special schools. The Warnock Report contrasts the attention given to teaching methods and pastoral care with the relative unconcern about curriculum in special schools and notes the danger that the schools may be too underdemanding in what they expect of their pupils. Though exceptions were found to these generalizations in some schools visited they remain as identified system weaknessses. If there is to be progress in all these areas in the future then the development of an A&SS in special education, as recommended in the Warnock Report, is essential. And planning to provide it is urgent in LEAs determined to develop the broader concept of special education.

Improving Discovery, Assessment and Placement

The main criticisms of discovery, assessment and placement concern the length of time taken to complete the process and the doubtful quality of some of the work. These are not new as they were directed at systems that operated before the Education Act 1981. At the same time it should be realized that there are examples of good procedures in the system and the problem is really one of finding ways to bring all LEAs nearer to the level of the best. Some features of good practice may be identified:

Hallmarks of Good Practice in LEAs.

(a) adequate professional staff—numbers and quality;
(b) easy relationships between schools, support services and administration;
(c) good communication and lack of rivalry between LEA, social services department, health authority and voluntary bodies;
(d) LEA and schools with 'open door' policies for parents and community;
(e) variety of special needs provision with special schools not isolated from ordinary schools;
(f) established and efficiently used consultative procedures in LEA.

The fact that the above qualities exist in some authorities (however few) takes them out of the realm of idealism and into that of the attainable. They are, therefore, objectives to be widely achieved if there is to be all-round improvement in the system.

But the common weaknesses cannot be ignored. We saw above

that much remains to be achieved in information for and relationships with parents of children with special needs. Many of the
difficulties are associated with the pre-school years and the early
stages of in-school assessment, both areas where communication
and cooperation are most important, and where failure can have
unfortunate effects on later procedures. Quite apart from the delay
that seems to be built into the system, failure of communication,
followed by lack of confidence in the authority by the parents,
appears to be a major factor in many prolonged assessments and
delays in agreement on placement. These points made, the system
is now examined in more detail.

Assessment

It would clearly be impossible to apply the interdisciplinary
assessment described in Chapter 2 to the one in five pupils whose
needs require assessment within the broader concept of special
education. And the fact is that for most of the pupils assessment at
that depth is not necessary. What is required, therefore, is a system
of assessment which will meet the needs of pupils whose special
education is possible within the arrangements of the ordinary
school with, where necessary, advice and guidance from the
supporting services. The first three stages of assessment outlined in
the Warnock Report (DES 1978, pp. 60–1) meet this need and have
been summarized in Chapter 2.

Stages one, two and three represent *in-school* assessment but the
LEA should ensure that adequate arrangements exist for carrying
out the procedures and monitoring their efficiency, particularly in
reviewing pupil progress. As indicated above, this task should form
an important part of the duties of the A&SS in the ordinary schools.
Some method of recording transactions at this level will be
necessary if the LEA is to be kept informed of the situation and data
are to be available on which to base the allocation of resources to the
schools.

Criticism of the Education Act 1981 has centred on the absence of
any attempt to establish procedures for the in-school assessments at
stages one to three, particularly as most pupils with special needs
will be assessed at these levels. The LEAs are left to decide for
themselves how they implement the Warnock Report suggestions
noted above. It is still open, of course, for the Secretary of State to
make regulations setting out basic procedures and minimum
standards for the procedures, though it will be difficult to do this in
any but the most general terms because of the variations that exist
among different schools.

Formal assessment (which forms the fourth stage or level) was also described in Chapter 2. Criticisms of the time taken over assessment usually refer to this stage and there appear to be two main reasons for delay. The first is the 'dead time' built into the process in the 1981 Act which is necessary in order to ensure that parents have adequate opportunity to make their contribution to assessment or question the LEA proposals. There seems to be some ambiguity in interpreting the Act. Some LEAs insist that the statutory times *must* elapse before the assessment can be moved on; others are prepared to move on before the time expires if parents are in agreement with proposals at that stage. This ambiguity should be cleared up and assessments should be moved forward without delay where there is parental agreement—taking the risk that parents may (as they have a right to) change their minds at a later stage. The second cause of delay rests on inefficient communication between the LEA and social services or health authority, or indeed both. There is reason to think that children in care, in hospital, or under hospital consultant care are at risk from this kind of delay. Where they exist, delays for these reasons call for a cooperative approach through joint courses for professionals, agreed joint guidelines of procedures, and a clear understanding by all concerned of the educational purpose of the assessment. Joint action by the DES and DHSS could give the necessary lead in this area of weakness.

However, it is in relation to parents that LEAs must act with wisdom and sensitivity. It cannot be assumed that all parents who require assistance in formulating representations or written evidence will approach the officer named as the source of further information. Many who need help may lack the initiative to seek it; others may be deterred by problems in expressing their opinions, particularly in writing. There is a moral if not a legal duty for LEAs to identify such parents, approach them with sensitivity and offer assistance in a manner calculated to secure its acceptance. Another complication arises from the assumption in the Act that assessment is a unitary process to be completed in one examination session. Only rarely are even the most straightforward assessments completed in such a manner and for some children it would be most unwise to subject them to that kind of arrangement. More typical are assessments where the different professional examinations are arranged in a phased manner considered suitable for the child and in places appropriate for the different examinations. If these cannot all be specified in the original notice to parents then a series of notices may be required. One thing is quite certain: children should not be scheduled in a manner which subordinates their needs to legal or administrative tidiness. Further, most of these problems will not arise if LEAs conduct their business in the spirit of the Warnock

Report as described in the account of stage one assessment and in the discussion of the parental role in assessment in Chapter 2, for parents involved in that manner will reach stage four with an understanding of their child's needs and the confidence in the LEA which grows out of knowledge and involvement.

It follows from the above that LEAs should be prepared to assist parents in contributing to assessment and many have devised effective procedures that should be more widely adopted. From those in use it is possible to derive general principles which help foster parental understanding and involvement:

Involving Parents in Assessment Procedures.

(a) readable letters that set out procedures clearly in an understandable and non-threatening manner;

(b) adaptation to the parent's language and culture when working with ethnic or cultural minorities;

(c) delivery of letters by a sympathetic and understanding person who can explain procedures clearly;

(d) continued personal contact and guidance where necessary;

(e) production of a straightforward pro forma to assist parents in making their contribution to assessment;

(f) where necessary, personalized assistance with the pro forma or with the formulation of written submissions;

(g) training in working with parents for LEA professionals and special needs staff in schools;

(h) understanding by all LEA staff involved that parents are likely to be under stress or at least anxious about the child;

(i) active fostering of parental involvement through willingness to modify procedures to accommodate parents.

Parents should be assisted in understanding that, just as formal assessment is not the beginning of the process for their child, neither is it the end. They should understand that the school in which the child may eventually be placed will continue to assess his needs and modify teaching to meet them, welcoming the parents as partners in the continuing assessment and in the special education of their child. They should also understand that assessment does in no way imply that placement will be in a special school. In developing this approach to assessment a valuable contribution has come from the development of parent profiles. (ILEA 1986; Wolfendale 1984).[7]

Placement

The Education Act 1981 imposes a duty on LEAs to educate children with special educational needs in ordinary schools wherever their special education can be made available in a manner compatible with the efficient education of other children and the efficient use of resources. The headteachers and governors of ordinary schools, in cooperation with the LEA, have a clear responsibility to provide efficient special teaching for those pupils who require it and to ensure that all teachers are aware of those children with special needs. How will these enactments affect the school placements of children with special educational needs? The situation is directly affected by the decision of the government that additional resources cannot be made available for the implementation of the Act; a decision which will make it extremely difficult to provide viable special educational situations within ordinary schools. Yet until such situations are provided, the problem of placing children with special needs in ordinary schools will remain essentially as described in Chapter 3. But there is a danger. Critics of the Act have pointed out that the omission of any attempt to define the minimum facilities to be provided for children with special needs in ordinary schools may encourage improper and ineffective provision in the absence of resources. If this should occur the problems facing those responsible for placement may be increased. These points made, it now remains to examine placement in more detail.

For most children with special educational needs it will not be necessary for the LEA to make a statement determining those needs. These are the children whose special needs have been successfully assessed at stages one to three and their special education is the direct responsibility of the headteachers and governors of the ordinary schools in which they will clearly remain. But the consequence of past neglect of special educational provision in ordinary schools is that among the above group are some children who rank as the most disadvantaged in the present educational system. If their education is to be both more appropriate and more efficient they need teachers with special training relevant to special needs who are supported by qualified and experienced advisers; they need more teachers so that they may learn in groups where they receive the individual attention which they require; they need specialized teaching materials which, at secondary level, will not be necessary for other pupils of the same age; and many require prolonged contact with individual teachers responsible for their learning, a fact which makes special demands on secondary school organization. These factors make demands on staffing and other facilities which are exceptionally difficult to provide within the present scale of resources and which cannot be provided on a wide scale without additional resources. At the same time there is contemporary evidence that resources in this area of education are being reduced. In response to central government pressure for reduced expenditure, some LEAs have reduced the number of remedial teachers available in the schools, or the provision of part-time teachers whose presence often contributed to the flexibility which enabled headteachers to make arrangements for special teaching, while delays in filling staff vacancies often penalize most those children with special needs as headteachers are forced to make temporary arrangements to cover vacancies. The erosion of school allowances through failure to keep them abreast of inflation creates further difficulty as the expensive equipment necessary for some children seems exceptionally expensive in relation to the number of children who require it. Yet this negative situation should not be allowed to deter attempts to make special provision within ordinary schools. There will be isolated situations (as at present) where conditions are conducive to efficient provision. These should be exploited whenever possible in order to extend the pool of experience and to demonstrate what is possible in suitable conditions, while, utilizing this experience, LEAs should involve their schools in planning developments to be implemented as facilities become available.

For the pupils with special educational needs determined by the LEA, those with a statement of special educational needs, their placement could be in special or ordinary school according to their needs. The placement required by a pupil will be indicated in part two of the statement of his needs, and where the conditions attached to placement in an ordinary school are satisfied it will be the duty of the LEA so to place the child. Once a child with special needs is placed in an ordinary school, the Act makes it the duty of those responsible for him to secure that he interacts as far as is practicable with pupils without special needs in the activities of the school. It will be difficult for governors and headteachers to discharge the responsibilities imposed upon them by the Act in relation to pupils for whom the LEA has made a statement of special educational needs without additional resources and special support from the LEA, while the pupils themselves are unlikely to benefit from placements made in the absence of satisfactory arrangements for their special education. If, as is generally expected, the Act gradually reduces the demand for places in special schools, then it may become possible to divert some existing resources into ordinary schools. But this is unlikely to resolve the whole problem or to be sufficiently rapid to satisfy those whose objective is integration as soon as possible. There is a danger here to which critics of the Act have pointed. These pupils require teachers with special training beyond that required for teaching pupils assessed at stages one to three; they have greater need for specialized equipment and health and social services support; they require an organization more distinct from that of the main school; and securing their interaction with other pupils generates special organizational pressures within the ordinary school. In these circumstances the absence in the Act or Regulations of any attempt to specify the minimum facilities to be provided in ordinary schools for pupils with needs determined by the LEA may put some pupils at risk by exposing them to hasty, ill-planned attempts at integration. These considerations should not deter LEAs from the search for conditions conducive to appropriate provision within ordinary schools and where they are identified they should be exploited, for only in this manner can the possibilities within ordinary schools be demonstrated in practical terms. There should also be forward planning to create suitable conditions or to identify where they may be created as facilities and resources become available. Officer time devoted to these activities will, in the final analysis, be more productive than short-term, insufficiently-considered attempts to move pupils with statements of special educational needs into inadequate or unsuitable ordinary school situations. It is necessary to remember always that there is more satisfaction to be gained from doing things well than from merely doing them first.

Reviews

We have seen that the LEA is required to review children with statements annually, between 13½ and 14½ years of age, and in certain circumstances when requested to do so by parents. These need not be full-scale formal reassessments, but they should include all teachers and other professionals working with the child and the child's parents. Where social services or the health authority are involved, special arrangements may be necessary to secure relevant contributions. It is for the review body to make any necessary recommendations concerning the child's progress or the support he requires; and, where necessary, they may require a formal reassessment of the child's special educational needs and placement. It is the responsibility of the LEA to organize a review system that includes recording and reporting to the authority. Ideally, the system should be part of authority policy for reviewing and recording the educational progress of all pupils in the schools.

Any efficient review system will make additional demands on education, social service and health authority staff, most of whom have a heavy load of other work. It is the same for parents, who must meet other family demands as well as earning a living. It follows, therefore, that the LEA must reduce demand to a minimum by careful planning. The more efficient the recording system as a cumulative record, the less time is involved in collecting information for reviews; the more the work can be spread throughout the year, the less the danger of gross overwork at any one time. Normal records designed so that they may be used directly in reviews reduce the additional written work to a minimum. Parents may require assistance with their contributions and with good planning this may become part of a routine visit by a social or welfare worker rather than the occasion of an extra call. Careful selection of children for review may be used to avoid overloading any one session with those likely to require prolonged discussion. These and similar simple procedures can keep the additional work within manageable limits. But the parents should take precedence throughout. They require ample notice, a time they can manage reasonably well, and the assistance noted above—and they should be made welcome as full and equal participants in the review.

Named person

As we have seen, the Education Act 1981 requires that parents of children with statements are given the name of a person from whom they may obtain information and advice about their child's needs and special education. But no role is attached to this person in the Act or in the Regulations. It is not surprising, therefore, as the Spastic Society Survey showed (Rogers 1986), that there is considerable variation among LEAs in relation to the role. The Warnock Report raised the question of the *named person* with a wide role as a facilitator for the family, but to some extent reduced the role by seeing the person as within the LEA for school-age children (DES 1978, pp. 76–8, 157–9). An ILEA survey found that there was a role for a named person, even to the extent of a family 'befriender' in some circumstances (ILEA 1986). The committee responsible for the report identified a need for the named person to be independent of the authority, possibly involving voluntary bodies or a panel of suitable people from which choice could be made. They also thought (and they are not alone in this) that the named person should be appointed early in the assessment process, when parents are anxious and uncertain, often in great need of information and impartial support. Of one thing they were both sure and correct. The role of the named person must to a large extent be shaped in interaction with the family, for family needs not only vary between families but within families in response to knowledge and experience. With that reservation, some principles of the role are identified.

Role of the Named Person.

(a) to direct parents to sources of information—interpreting if necessary;

(b) as enabler—encouraging negotiation—avoiding confrontation unless essential,

(c) as a direct link with LEA—encouraging interaction, acting on behalf of parents if necessary;

(d) as liasion person with other statutory bodies and voluntary agencies—obtaining information and fostering contact;

(e) to act as friend and counsellor to the family—especially in the early stages of assessment and placement.

Because family needs differ, consideration of the named person could become part of the assessment process. The needs of some might be met by an officer of the authority—another may need a fully independent person. But to make a reality of the role requires action by the LEA. The local community must be alerted to the role as offering a worthwhile outlet for voluntary service; suitable people must be recruited to form a panel from which selection may be made; there must be some training to prepare them for the role; and they will require a basic administration to allow them to concentrate on the work with families. Training and orientation could become a task for the Advisory Service for Special Needs while the special education administration offer the necessary organizational support. The enterprise requires careful handling. Too close an identification with the LEA would detract from the value of the named person to parents most in need of impartial support while a role too remote might deprive a named person of essential support and information. An alternative arrangement might be for an existing voluntary body to take on the organization and training role with a budgetary and training input from the LEA if necessary.

Summary

The responsibilities of LEAs are reviewed together with progress in implementing the Education Act 1981. There are two sets of opinion, optimistic and pessimistic. Basic concerns are summarized and balanced by reference to positive features in the system. Differences between the Warnock Report (DES 1978) and the Education Act 1981 are identified and compared with the suggestion that the former offers the better guide towards a broader concept of special education. Resources, teacher training, local cooperation, regional organization and planning problems are reviewed and it is concluded that there is a movement towards implementation though it is slow while showing some positive features. Criticisms of assessment and placement are identified and there are suggestions for improving the process[8], in particular parental involvement. Finally the role of the *named person* is examined with suggestions for further development.

Notes

1. The views represented here are subjective. Sources are colleagues involved in special education at all levels in widely spread parts of the country. Generalizations based upon conversations and letters have been further tested in discussion with different people. As far as is possible the generalizations reflect a concensus of the opinions received.
2. National Union of Teachers, NAS/UWT, National Association for Remedial Education, National Council for Special Education, Spastics Society, Advisory Centre for Education.
3. Mainly the abolition of Area Health Authorities and the reorganization of District Health Authorities but also financial difficulties and the reallocation of funds by DHSS.
4. The average seems to be about two years.
5. From April 1983, pupils then in special schools were assumed to have statements. LEAs were given a year to carry out reassessments of these pupils (not necessarily full formal procedures) making statements where judged necessary.
6. Information from Mary Hope, Micro-electronics Programme National Co-ordinator for Special Needs, Council for Educational Technology, 3 Devonshire Street, London W1N 2BA.
7. Parent profiles are designed to present the parents perception of the child in the home and their views on the childs special education. The Fish Committee (ILEA 1986) found them well received when introduced to parents.
8. There seems to be some conflicting advice on statements between LEAs and District Health Authorities. The DES requires LEAs to put the child's needs first; the DHSS advises DHAs to consider resource availability. The Society of Education Officers is seeking clarification through a joint DES–DHSS statement. See *Education*, 16 May 1986, p. 445.

References

Department of Education and Science (1978), *Special Educational Needs* (Warnock Report), Cmnd. 7212, HMSO.
DES (1985a), *Better Schools*, Cmnd. 9469, HMSO.
DES (1985b), *Proposed New Specific Grant Arrangements for In-service Education of Teachers*, HMSO.
Holt, M. (1986), 'One Step Forward, Two Steps Back', *Education*, 20 June.

Inner London Education Authority (1986), *Educational Opportunities For All* (Fish Report), ILEA, Chapter 13.

Mittler, P. (1986), 'New Look in In-service Training', *British Journal of Special Education*, vol. 13, no. 2.

Rogers, R. (1986), *Caught in the Act*, Centre for Studies on Integration in Education/Spastics Society.

Wolfendale, (1984), 'Parental Profiling and Parental Contributions to Assessment and Statementing', North-East London Polytechnic, Dept of Psychology.

CHAPTER 5

Development in the Means of Special Education

The means of special education are those situations in which the child or young person with special educational needs is in an appropriate learning environment supervised by a teacher with relevant training or experience, or both. It is here that the quality of special education is determined. If the potential of the broader concept of special education is to be realized then developments in these means of education will be necessary, not only in schools and colleges, but in other situations where teachers and learners come together. This chapter anticipates some of the necessary developments.

Pre-School Developments

The point has been made that the disabilities which are obvious at birth or in the early years are those which are obtrusive or interfere with primary functions in the young child. The need for early intervention and family support is recognized and provided mainly from the health and social services. The need for early educational intervention is a more recent development, it is not widely available and is usually limited to children with major sensory loss or severe mental handicap. This work requires development and extension. Language disorder or delay, social deprivation and lack of intellectual stimulation are now recognized as conditions which generate special educational needs and can create problems in education in later years. Similar problems arise when physical disabilities and delayed motor activities limit experience critical for perceptual and intellectual growth. To eliminate or reduce the effect of these conditions a general enrichment programme is required, but it needs to be supported by the definition of critical learning objectives and the design and execution of structured activities directed at their achievement. With young children the latter activities make great demands on resources because of the need for individual teaching in a one-to-one situation, and the teacher requires training and insight in order to maintain a correct balance between enrichment and structure. The main problem is that of providing the necessary manpower for the development and extension of pre-school educational intervention.

Consideration of the above problem led to the concept of the parents as the child's first educator. Though valid for all young children, the idea is of special importance for those children at risk of educational failure, as it is just those children who have greatest need for the insights of a teacher trained in special education and experienced with pre-school children. However, if the training and experience of the teacher can be exercised through the involvement of the parents, making use of their natural intimacy with their child, then maybe the problem of manpower could be resolved. This is the starting point for the work of pre-school home teachers working within the Advisory and Support Service in special education and a first task is to extend and develop their work, placing emphasis on work with the child as an opportunity to involve the parents in the child's education and shape their contribution.

But the education of the parents extends beyond their actual work with their child. They must be made aware of and introduced to other agencies of support such as day nurseries, nursery schools or classes, playgroups, opportunity groups, toy libraries, parents' workshops and voluntary organizations. A special role for the home teacher is to inform the parents about and establish their contact with the special education situations which the child may need in later years. These wider aspects of the work cannot be carried out by the teacher unaided. At many points she will cooperate with other workers from the health and social services, and from the voluntary organizations working with handicapped children and their families. The fact is that effective intervention in the pre-school years cannot be sustained by the education service alone. The next necessary development, therefore, is an organized cooperative approach to the pre-school education of children and parents which involves the three local services and the relevant voluntary workers. Models already exist in the 'Portage' project and the Hampshire replications of it, and these could be linked with Boxall's nurture group approach in the schools.

The two approaches complement each other. In Portage, project workers are trained to work with the parents of handicapped children in the pre-school years and in the child's home. Emphasis is on assisting the parent to recognize and set appropriate learning objectives for the child and to interact with the child, assisting him to achieve the objectives. Thus the parent becomesthe child's first teacher, and about 60 per cent of those involved appear to have been successful. Health visitors, social workers and pre-school teachers, as well as voluntary workers, all have a part in this type of approach. On the other hand the nurture group, as developed in ILEA, is based in the infant school or early years of the infant and junior school. The objective is to establish a classroom regime which recaptures as far as possible the ethos of pre-school years in the home, attempting to provide the critical experiences for children deprived of them through social or cultural inadequacy or deviance. Many home-like activities feature in the work and there is special emphasis on food and cooperative dining. Combinations of these approaches could link home and school for young children with special needs; they offer opportunities for cooperation between the services and voluntary effort; and in times of financial stringency may be the means of expanding facilities within limited budgets (DES 1978, pp. 80–93; Boxall 1976; ILEA 1986). As former 'remedial' services are transformed into Advisory Services for Special Needs, work at pre-school level tends to expand, taking advantage of the clearer LEA responsibilities and improved communications with the Health Service. This is not evident in all LEAs and even those moving in the pre-school years appear to be restricted by limitation of resources, though the DES has allocated £1.2 million to establish Portage-type schemes during 1986–7. While Portage schemes have been slow to expand, it is noticeable that many of the positive features have been incorporated in the less structured work of pre-school home teachers, mainly because they are consistent with the Warnock Report principle of the parent as the child's first educator.

Development in Ordinary Schools

Discovering special needs

The first task of development in the ordinary schools must be to ensure that children with special educational needs are discovered as early as possible so that arrangements may be made to meet their needs and increase the probability of their full participation in mainstream education; or where that is not possible, have max-imum exposure to the special education which they require. The development of teacher training noted in Chapter 4, if effectively applied, should secure an extension of sensitive awareness of and knowledge about special educational needs in the schools. As a result, teachers should become aware of early signs of emerging difficulties and be more skilled in resolving them at a stage where they are amenable to ordinary classroom approaches. In itself this will bring about some reduction in the number of children put forward for further assessment. This is seen in those LEAs that have developed well-structured observation schemes with the schedules incorporated in ongoing classroom activities, assessment and record-keeping.[1] Other LEAs have developed whole-year surveys of the school population on a continuing annual basis. The most critical survey is that between the ages of 7 and 8. Here pupils with mild and moderate learning difficulties begin to reveal their inadequacies in formal learning, and they form the largest group of pupils who require special education. The objective is to devise simple group tests of intellectual level and attainment and a behaviour checklist which will identify the majority of pupils with acceptable learning and behaviour. Those not cleared by the survey are then considered for assessment at the appropriate stage if they have not already been detected and assessed. Of the pupils so identified, some will have their special needs met through modifications in the ordinary schools, others will require assessment at stage four with, possibly, a statement by the LEA and placement in special schools or designated special classes. It should be noted that the Warnock Committee recommended this type of approach (DES 1978, p. 56) and the development is one which does not require government legislation.

Though both the above approaches have value and improve the situation in LEAs adopting them, a comprehensive scheme should incorporate features of each. The survey ensures that all pupils are scrutinized and reduces the possibility of any being overlooked; also, by limiting the number to be examined in depth, it makes for a more manageable situation. Observation schedules ensure that all children are regularly reviewed and allow careful monitoring of those with real or emerging special educational needs. They also identify pupils whose special needs begin to develop after the annual survey.

Special needs without statements

Ordinary schools have a responsibility to maintain proper records and reviews of pupils assessed at stages one to three who are not the subject of a statement by the LEA but are receiving special education in the school. Parents should be involved at each point and made fully aware of any changes in the arrangements made for their child and a common recording system in the authority should provide information valuable in planning and distributing resources. The school records should form the basis for reviews that define the changing special educational needs of individual pupils and propose the measures necessary to meet them. But the measures will be effective only in schools that have developed a wide range of options to meet a variety of learning needs or provide non-teaching support where necessary.

Options within the ordinary school.

(a) Class/subject teacher advised by more experienced colleague.

(b) Class/subject teacher advised by the head of special needs.

(c) Class/subject teacher advised by visiting advisory teacher for special needs.

(d) Advice from (a), (b) or (c), supported by teaching material suitable for the pupil(s) concerned.

(e) Any of the above derived from the school special needs resource centre where one exists.

(f) Teachers from (a), (b), (c) or (e) working with the pupil(s) and class/subject teacher in the ordinary classroom.

(g) Changes to pupils' timetable, subjects or teachers.

(h) Pupil(s) withdrawn for special teaching as individuals or in small group, or in special class.

(i) Arrangements for special preparation or follow-up to maintain pupil(s) in the ordinary situation.

(j) Consultation with educational psychologist—advice input into any of the above situations.

(k) Necessary non-teaching support arranged in ordinary classroom or in withdrawn situation.

(l) Consultation with head of appropriate special school for advice.

(m) Input from special school—outreach teacher to ordinary school or pupil(s) for special school session(s).

(n) Pupil(s) placed in special class in ordinary school with regulated interaction with mainstream class.

(o) At any point above, modification of the curriculum to be followed by the pupil.

It is the responsibility of the headteacher to see that the options are established and properly used, though in many schools he will delegate this to a specially qualified member of staff who will be supported by the A&SS. Inputs from the health and social services may be required among the options. One thing is certain: special education in ordinary schools will not be a reality until the necessary options are available and are used in a flexible manner to meet special educational needs in children.

Special needs with statements

The operation of the Education Act 1981 has the effect of making ordinary schools responsible for the education of some children with special educational needs determined through a statement by the LEA. Whatever their special needs such pupils form three main groups. First are those children who are capable of following the normal curriculum if they have the non-teaching support made necessary by their disabilities. An example would be an intelligent physically handicapped pupil requiring support in order to move around the school. The second group is formed from those pupils who require special teaching or curriculum in some areas but are able to participate in normal curriculum to a limited extent. Some pupils with physical disability, health problems or moderate learning difficulties would be in this group, with, possibly, pupils with emotional or behaviour difficulties able to participate in some normal classes if adequately supported at other times. The third group consists of pupils who require separate teaching because of extensive sensory loss, the need for extensively modified curriculum or specialized teaching methods, or major modifications in the size or tone of the basic teaching group, but who may, nevertheless, gain substantially from social interaction in the school. The groups are not exclusive: for instance, a pupil in the second group may require the mobility assistance suggested by the example of the first group during his limited participation in normal curriculum. Examples of possible arrangements for these groups may be worked out from the list in Chapter 3, and it would be interesting to consider how the pupils described in Chapter 1 could be placed in the situations listed. Molly, for instance, is receiving full-time education in ordinary classes with periods of withdrawal to a special unit for support. John is in a similar situation except that the support he needs because of his physical condition is provided within his ordinary school. Bertie attends a day special school as a full-time pupil but has intermittent social contact with normal pupils on occasional visits to an ordinary school or with pupils from those schools who assist in Bertie's special school. At present Anne is a full-time pupil in a residential special school and her social contacts with normality are limited to out-of-school situations. Barry has most of his teaching in a special class in his ordinary school but he has full social contact within the school and limited contact with teaching in ordinary classes. The opportunities for pupils with special educational needs to interact with children without such needs should be greatly increased by the development and extension of designated special units and classes within ordinary schools.

Designated classes or units

Unlike the ordinary special classes, which may be organized by headteachers to meet the needs of pupils on the school roll who are not the subject of a statement by the LEA but require special education, designated classes or units will normally be established on the initiative of the LEA. Children should not be placed in designated classes except after interdisciplinary assessment at stage four followed by a statement of special educational needs: in other words, the pupils will have been assessed in the same manner as pupils placed in special schools. The difference will be that part III of the statement has indicated placement in a designated class or unit as being the appropriate situation to meet their special educational needs. A designated class or unit will, therefore, admit any pupil for whom it is suitable, *irrespective* of whether or not he is on the roll of the host ordinary school. The designated situation will become the base in which pupils who are the subject of a statement by the LEA receive their special teaching, special curriculum or counselling in connection with their special educational needs. But it must be more than that. The whole purpose of the situation is to create opportunity for interaction between pupils with special needs and other pupils in the school, whether in teaching, social activities or both. The degree to which this is organized for the individual pupil must be determined by the pupil's needs, though the organization will require close cooperation between the teacher in charge of the designated situation, the headteacher of the school and the teachers who receive into their classes pupils from the designated class or unit. Apart from consideration of the special education of the pupils, designated classes or units must conform as much as possible to the routine of the school, teachers will be full members of the school staff and teachers and pupils should participate in all appropriate extra-curricular activities. A special education adviser should have a continuing association with the special education teachers and pupils and should ensure that a balance is kept between special needs and wider school involvement. Interaction of staff, unit teachers doing some work in the school and schoolteachers in the unit, is a sign of a mature situation and should be fostered, while unit teachers should also maintain contact with an appropriate special school so that they do not lose contact with developments in special schools. Indeed, if this link is fostered, it could provide important back-up for the designated unit with opportunities for interchange of staff.

School resource centre for special needs

Designated classes or units in the above terms are consistent with the recommendations of the Warnock Report; they are beginning to develop in some schools and have been observed operating successfully for blind, deaf and partially hearing, physically disabled pupils and pupils with moderate and severe learning difficulties. But there is a tendency for them to be somewhat self-contained, offering little support for wider school problems though some pupils may have limited teaching in ordinary classes. Though this is a useful beginning and not to be neglected, the presence in a school of specialized teachers and facilities could be developed into a wider role with beneficial effect on a wide range of school activities. It involves a bringing together of the options discussed above for in-school provision and their combination with the more specialist function of the designated class in a comprehensive school resource centre for special educational needs.

Such a resource centre should reach out into almost every aspect of the life of the school. It supports widely the frequently discussed concept of a 'whole-school' approach to special needs. It supports pupils, however severe their disability, who can follow normal school curriculum if provided with the necessary educational and non-educational assistance—either providing it directly or organizing its input from local statutory services. The resource base itself is the fall-back for pupils whose exposure to normal teaching or curriculum must be limited because of their disability, or because they require additional preparation or follow-up if they are to maintain their place within it. Homework sessions in school for socially disadvantaged or culturally deviant pupils become part of resource centre responsibility. Pupils with more serious special needs, those with major sensory disability, or those requiring major alteration in the size or tone of teaching group may have most of their teaching in special classes or groups associated with the resource centre, though with appropriate regulated exposure to mainstream activities, teaching or both. It is not impossible that, given the facilities, the resource centre could accept some pupils who would receive all their teaching within it yet gain considerable benefit from interaction with the wider activities of the ordinary school. It *is* possible to have a special school within an ordinary school—and that without isolation. All that has been lacking up to now has been the will and the resources.

To operate as suggested above a comprehensive resource centre for special needs must be organized in consistency with certain basic assumptions which, no doubt, will require refinement through experience:

School Resource Centre for Special Needs
Basic Assumptions

(a) The ascertained needs of individual pupils determine the balance of centre/mainstream teaching and curriculum.

(b) This balance will be different for different pupils and will be reflected in personal timetables.

(c) All staffing, equipment and capitation for the centre should be additional to the normal allocations for the school.

(d) Core staff of the centre will be available for consultation by all mainstream colleagues on any problem at any level.

(e) Specialized teaching materials developed through the centre are available to assist all mainstream colleagues.

(f) Core staff of the centre will teach with colleagues in ordinary classrooms where this is considered advisable.

(g) The centre will be the point of contact with appropriate special schools and the Special Needs Advisory Service.

(h) As they gain confidence and experience mainstream staff will be encouraged to participate in resource centre teaching.

(i) The core staff of the resource centre are available as a special needs in-service facility for the school.

The comprehensive resource centre as described should be able to organize and provide for a wide range of special needs within the school but in specialized areas a role may be allocated by the LEA. Some special educational needs demand equipment or accommodation not easily provided within ordinary classrooms and which it would be uneconomic to duplicate in too many ordinary schools. In this category come some of the requirements for teaching pupils with visual impairment, hearing loss, physical disabilities restricting mobility, combined physical and mental handicap, and extreme forms of emotional or behavioural disorder. It may well be that a comprehensive resource centre would be restricted to providing for only one group of the above disabilities, at least in extreme form. Table 5.1 illustrates the facilities required in a resource centre for different disabilities. In general it is desirable that the centre should share the facilities of the main school wherever possible in order to reduce separation even for the most severely disabled children. The decision, however, must remain with the staff concerned and there are two imperatives. First, there must be respect for the privacy and dignity of the pupils with disabilities, and second, where space is shared it *must* be capable of containing the increased usage without loss of civilized amentities. But if there is to be worthwhile interaction then the facilities of ordinary classrooms in the school will require evaluation, particularly where they are to accommodate children with visual or hearing disabilities or severe physical limitations. It is not enough that classrooms with suitable space, lighting or acoustic features are provided in the resource centre: there must be sufficient treated classrooms in the school to ensure that curriculum restrictions are not imposed upon pupils through accommodation inadequacies.

Table 5.1   Resource centre facilities for different disabilities

	Physical	Severe Learning	Visual	Hearing	Emotional Behaviour	Health	Moderate Learning
Two/three teaching spaces	√	√	√	√	√	√	√
Open interaction space	√	√	√	√	√	√	×
Visitors room/specialists	√	√	√	√	√	×	×
Special medical room	√	√	×	×	×	√	×
Physiotherapy space/store	√	√	×	×	×	×	×
Office/clerical facility	√	√	√	√	√	√	√
Special toilet/hygiene	√	√	×	×	×	×	×
Special vehicle access	√	√	×	×	×	×	×
Access all classrooms	√	×	√	√	√	√	√
Special sensory equipment	×	√	√	√	×	×	×
Rest/withdrawal space	√	√	×	×	√	√	×

Note: √ = Facility required.   × = Probably not required. That a facility is indicated as required does not imply separate provision as it may be possible to share the main facilities of the school.

Given the above facilities, staffing of a resource centre should be related to any specialized role allocated to it by the LEA. The number of teaching spaces must be taken into account along with the fact that, if the centre is to have its proper function in the school, a high proportion of teaching by centre staff will be in ordinary classrooms supporting colleagues. Furthermore, if advice is to have a sound basis, then time must be allowed for observation of problem situations in the school. A reasonable level for teaching staff would be that of an appropriate special school plus an additional teacher. Similar considerations apply to non-teaching staff. They, too, must work out in ordinary classrooms and assisting movement in the large ordinary school will make more demand than in a small special school. Both groups, if the centre becomes truly integrated as anticipated, will have more demands on their time from out-of-class activities than would be expected in a special school. On the basis of three teaching spaces the pupil and staffing levels of Table 5.2 seem reasonable. The pupils are those with special needs determined by the LEA through a statement at a level which, in the absence of the resource centre, would have indicated placement in a special school—as a working guide they might require to be in the resource centre for 50–60 per cent of their time in school. Pupils spending less than 50 per cent of their time in the support centre should not be counted in its numbers but regarded as a support problem in mainstream.

Table 5.2   *Pupils and staff in a comprehensive support centre*

Disability	Pupils	Teachers	Non-teachers
Hearing loss	15	4	2
Visual loss	18	4	4
Emotion/behaviour	18	4	2
Physical	21	4	4
Health	24	4	2
Severe learning	25	4	4
Moderate learning	33	4	2

In developing special educational needs provision in ordinary schools to meet the requirements of the Education Act 1981 and the long-term objectives of the Warnock Report there is probably a need for a support centre similar to the one outlined in every secondary school and large primary school. The objective is to create a situation in the ordinary school that allows efficient provision for the widest possible range of special needs. To that must be added the objective of flexibility to accommodate a range between the mild temporary need recognized in the school and the severe permanent need determined by the LEA in a statement. Such a resource centre satisfies two necessary criteria. On one hand it covers the range of Warnock integration—locational, social and functional. On the other hand it covers the DES range of curriculum—mainstream with support, modified and developmental. But to satisfy these desirable objectives there must be a planned whole-school policy on interaction by pupils and staff that is clear in concepts and operation, involving the total staff, the governors and the parents. It should also be communicated to the community served by the school.

The management for special needs

Providing appropriate education for pupils with special needs *not* determined by the LEA in statements will form the larger part of special education in the ordinary schools and new standards of teaching and monitoring will extend school responsibilities. Added to the task in some schools will be the responsibilities generated by designated classes or units for pupils whose special educational needs *are* determined in a statement by the LEA. Organizing interaction within the school, extended contributions from members of supportive services and the clerical work demanded by the new responsibilities will generate management problems in comprehensive schools and in the larger primary schools. Timetabling designated unit pupils in ordinary classes, reviewing their progress and advising their ordinary teachers, making arrangements for multi-professional review when required, responding to approaches from their parents about their education and developing that part of their special education provided in the designated unit will create new professional tasks within the school. The total of these duties, in both extent and complexity, forms a daunting task and it is doubtful if an existing organization based upon 'slow learners' or 'remedial' departments will prove adequate in the new situation. A fresh approach is required. The starting point could be the concept of all-embracing special education in the school centred upon the specialist teachers in the designated unit but with implications and involvements reaching into every department or class in the school and making a contribution to overall school policy. To direct this a head of special education will be necessary. It is not advisable that the head of special education should head a department or lead a faculty, for the responsibilities of the post extend into every part of the school where children with special needs pose problems for their teachers. What is needed is a special education team. The group of special education teachers form the support base on which the head of special education may draw in arranging advice for colleagues and special teaching for pupils at any level and they should be the start of the resource facility in the school. But more is required if the new situation is to be fully exploited. The head of special education should lead a working group in the school which includes an interested teacher from every department or faculty in a secondary school or from each year level in a large primary school. Each would become the point of interaction between their colleagues and the working group bringing suggestions, ideas and problems for discussion. They would identify information and support required by their colleagues, consult on curriculum and teaching methods for children with special needs and when necessary secure inputs to department, faculty or year-group meetings. At the same time each member of the working group should participate in the formulation of school policy relative to pupils with special needs for submission to academic board or staff council as appropriate. In time there should be at least one member of every section of the school well informed about the place of special education in the school and the teaching of children with special needs in their own area of curriculum. A later development would be to train interested teachers from the subject areas of the school in special teaching and to formulate a role for them in the resource facility so that it may become a resource centre drawing from and contributing to every area of the school. To be effective in the leadership role the head of special education must be more than a specialist teacher of children with special needs. Other professional and personal qualities are required such as: wide interests outside the school, a broad background in education, association with a range of school activities, a friendly but firm personality, and professional competence the equal of other senior members of the school staff. It would be appropriate to write such a person into the school senior management team at a level just below that of the deputy headteacher.

Neighbourhood placements

A neighbourhood placement policy is one in which, whenever possible, a child with special educational needs is admitted to the local school—the one which would have been attended in the absence of special needs. Facilities to meet the special needs are made available to the school. The most attractive feature of these placements is the retention of the child in the local community and the closeness of friends and family, while in the situations observed the warmth of relationships in the schools was impressive. Most of the children with special needs had physical disabilities (some quite severe), moderate learning difficulties or health problems but they were accepted as full members of the school communities by other pupils and staff and their education appeared to be proceeding at an acceptable level. Teachers had taken considerable effort to inform themselves about the needs of the pupils (sometimes with less direct help than desirable from their Authority) and non-teaching assistants were also of good quality. Only a few parents were seen but they expressed satisfaction with the schools and support for the policy.

The policy seems to be most suitable where schools are small and the development of a resource centre difficult, for instance in rural areas of small primary schools separated by distances that preclude a grouping approach. In such situations even day special schools may be ruled out by problems of transport and inconvenience to pupils and families. These were, in fact, the circumstances in which the policies were observed to be working well, to the extent that pupils with physical disabilities who once would have been placed in a distant boarding school were receiving good quality primary education in their local school.

Based upon the situations observed, there appear to be certain features necessary for a successful neighbourhood policy:

Essentials for Successful Neighbourhood Placement.

(a) Open and early discussion of proposals with parents and local community.
(b) Thorough briefing and preparation of the schools staffs.
(c) Organization of additional teaching support (staff, advisors, etc.) and integration with existing staff.
(d) Appointment of necessary non-teaching staff and organization of necessary input from health or social service departments.
(e) Completion of any necessary alterations to classrooms.
(f) Provision of any necessary toilet or hygiene facilities.
(g) Arrangements for additional capitation.
(h) Arrangements for any necessary contacts with clinics, hospitals, special schools, etc.

These may seem formidable requirements at first sight but in practice prove manageable. Many special needs (moderate learning difficulties, emotional or behaviour difficulties, health problems, etc.) make few structural demands other than the basic one of space. Even for serious physical disabilities structural alterations for accommodation seem relatively minor. It has to be remembered that these disabilities are thinly spread in the community; in a neighbourhood policy it is unlikely that any primary school would ever have more than two or three such pupils on roll. The opening out of a toilet, replacement of a washbasin with a sluice, a partition to make a changing area, the setting aside of a corner of a hall for physiotherapy, and ramps around the school seemed to have created satisfactory conditions. This is not to dismiss the problems to be resolved, nor to suggest that there should be any neglect of essentials or civilized conditions. But it does prompt a dangerous thought about the elaborate facilities we provide in special schools for children with physical disabilities and come to regard as essential. Are the elaborate facilities required by the disabilities of individual pupils? Or are they necessary because we have insisted on bringing together in the one place *large numbers* of pupils with physical disabilities?

Two points are noted which may be important. First, in the schools concerned falling rolls had removed the pressure on space and created conditions favourable to the development. Second, success was more evident at primary than at secondary level. In the way our education system operates pupils concentrate in numbers at secondary level and this also applies to those with special needs. Consequently the special needs numbers in secondary schools were much higher than in primary schools and the level of facilities less than adequate. There was, it seemed, a need for a resource approach such as described above. It would have improved the situation for the special needs group and contributed to the solution or easing of many other problems in the schools. Also, as communications between the secondary school and the contributing primary schools are already established, a secondary resource centre might well contribute to the primary cluster.

Campus sites

A campus site brings together special and ordinary schools in a proximity intended to facilitate interaction between pupils and staffs. The isolation of the special school is eliminated or reduced, the pupils in the ordinary schools have contact with pupils with special needs and they, in turn, are closer to normality, and the staffs should gain from added insight into each other's problems. Or so the advocates would have it. What is certain is that much good planning is necessary if the objectives are to be achieved, for it is possible for schools on campus to remain relatively separate, failing to exploit their situation.

One campus observed was successful by any standard— particularly on interaction with its companion comprehensive school. Good relations prevailed between the headteachers and staffs of the schools; a high proportion of the pupils with physical disabilities were in the secondary school for some part of their curriculum—the degree regulated by the needs and potential of individuals; and pupils reaching a point of majority teaching in the secondary school were transferred to the roll of that school. One point noted was the easy relationship between special school pupils and secondary school staff which seemed to be a carry-over from the excellent relationships in the special school.

Subsequently, as the teachers concerned gained experience and developed confidence, a further development took place. Motivated by extraneous developments that need not concern us here, the headteachers promoted the idea of a specialized unit to be part of the comprehensive school and provide for senior pupils with special needs. The idea was taken on by the LEA, the unit accommodation created in space made available by the falling roll in the comprehensive school, and a senior member of the special school staff moved over to head the unit. The space released in the special school will be used to rehouse a nursery unit currently in a hospital. Assessing the development, the headteacher of the special school rates it successful with only minor reservations. But more important, he indicates that he would have had doubts about the move in the early days of his campus experience and only came to favour it on the basis of what was achieved as the campus developed. This seems a good example of the creative use of experience.

In some situations the campus idea may have much to offer but there are difficulties. Large sites needed may be difficult to obtain and even impossible in urban areas where they may also be prohibitively expensive. Success requires planning of a very high order and careful selection of staffs for all the schools to achieve a balance that may be difficult to sustain over long periods. While the campus can be successful where the situation is particularly suitable, it is unlikely to become a major feature in the future development of special education.

Random placements

What we choose to call random placements do not constitute a development as such but more a situation in schools commented upon more often than desirable. In this situation there seems to be no rational plan or principle regulating placements other than the uncritical acceptance that pupils with special educational needs determined through a statement should be placed in ordinary schools. Pupil's needs appear to be considered in isolation from the situation in which they are to be educated, with little thought given to the particular schools involved, their possibilities or their potential. The schools concerned found statements unhelpful because of the absence of detailed information and we were told that bald statements like 'Ordinary school with two half-hours weekly of additional teaching' were not unusual. Frequently, it was asserted, advisers or even schools were left to their own resources in finding the additional teaching. Headteachers reported staff frustration and pupil detriment where long periods elapsed between admission of the pupil and the appearance of the specified assistance. There were suggestions that some unsatisfactory statements resulted from undue parental pressure and recommendations made primarily to secure parental agreement. One extreme case was reported where the statement specified the exact teaching method to be used in the classroom that had been dictated by a parent. Interestingly, the receiving school had no knowledge of the method. We have no absolute proof of these situations and rely on the integrity of those reporting them; nor is it suggested that they represent the normal situation. What is suggested is that their presence at any level is unacceptable.

Development in Special Schools

Special schools have a long history as a means of providing education for handicapped pupils in Britain. In its evidence to the Warnock Committee the largest education authority, ILEA, affirmed that 'in many respects, the special school represents a highly developed technique of positive discrimination', and the weight of evidence supported their continuation alongside movement into ordinary schools. The committee concluded that there was a continuing role for special schools in the new system of special education, and the Education Act 1981 secures their future. Nevertheless change is inevitable. The prevailing ethos which questions the wisdom of separating handicapped pupils from their fellows, the extension of provision for special education in ordinary schools, and the fall in the school population will threaten some individual special schools and require adaptation to a new situation for those which remain. But change is slow and gradual, as indicated by the data in Chapter 1. The school population is only now reaching its predicted low and moves into ordinary schools make demands on resources and training that are difficult to meet in prevailing circumstances. As demand for teachers falls off in special schools their skill and experience should be in demand for the designated situations in the ordinary schools, two features to be considered by those who plan the changes.

There is also the possibility of further changes in the pattern of disabilities which affect children. Extension and improvement in genetic counselling, more sophisticated diagnosis in early pregnancy allied to termination, improved obstetrics and pre- and post-natal care may both reduce handicaps and change their pattern. Against this must be set the current run-down of the health and social services which results from government policy of minimal expenditure allied to the effect of inflation; the lowering in extent and quality of the school meal service for similar reasons; and the scale of unemployment which could lead to the reappearance of nutritional diseases to the elimination of which the school meals service made a significant contribution.

The effect of the changes on the special schools can be predicted with reasonable confidence. After a slow start in which there will be little movement away from special schools a quickening of change will show, initially involving pupils who are capable of following the normal school curriculum if provided with appropriate support. This will be followed by the movement into ordinary schools of pupils who require a modified curriculum. The pace of change will be regulated by the resources made available in ordinary schools and in particular to the development of special needs resource centres. In this interim period interaction between special and ordinary schools should accelerate. The resource centres will have need for special schools expertise; some special schools will become 'resource centres' themselves servicing ordinary school situations as they provide 'out reach' teachers for resource centres and neighbourhood placements. But gradually expertise will be acquired in ordinary schools closely related to their specific circumstances; school resource centres may take over the outreach function of the special schools and the input from the latter may be affected by falling demand. Meanwhile special schools will become fewer in number, have smaller rolls, larger catchment areas and a school population nearer the extreme of serious and complex special educational needs. They will find it necessary to develop new approaches to their problems and their experience will become less immediately relevant to the circumstances of ordinary schools. Some of these changes are discussed later, but first a comment on falling school rolls.

Schools and school rolls

Because there will be fewer special schools, the location of those which remain will be critical. Links with families, transport of pupils to school, input from health and social services will all require evaluation in relation to school location. The size of roll will raise questions of curriculum validity in many schools. Yet this must be seen against the changes in intake, for the curriculum may be more circumscribed by the needs of seriously and multiply handicapped pupils. These factors may be offset if the broader grouping of needs results in a lifting of school roll, though this itself may reintroduce the question of curriculum viability. Questions of curriculum viability may also be affected by interaction with ordinary schools, discussed below. Some of these questions will raise the issue of the extent to which designated units or resource centres are capable of providing education for seriously or multiply handicapped pupils. At present there is little experience on which to base answers to such questions, but conditions may require continuous evaluation of them as experience extends. In rural areas there may be an early, forced choice between neighbourhood placements, designated units or boarding provision.

Serious and complex disabilities

It is an open question whether providing for a limited range of complex or serious disabilities is a more difficult task than educating the same children in a school where the other children range to the near-normal. The only certain thing is that both problems are difficult, though different. The limited population of the future special school will allow teachers to concentrate on the specialized curricula and teaching methods required by a narrow range of serious or complex handicaps. Curriculum objectives will be more easily defined, equipment and materials more closely related to the task, method more carefully shaped to the needs of the pupils, support inputs more specifically related to needs, and the purpose of the school explained to parents and the community with greater clarity. On the other hand, deviation from the ordinary school will increase. The balance of education and care in the schools will change; consequently the role of teachers will be subtly affected; educational progress by the children may be relatively slow, requiring finer definitions of sub-goals or objectives or the postulation of learning objectives over an unrealistic period of time; while teaching and learning situations form a smaller proportion of the school day. The needs of the pupils may dictate a pattern of school day and school year which introduces another deviation from the normal pattern of schools. In many schools medical and paramedical needs will impose greater constraints on education, affecting more pupils and requiring more of their time away from the classroom, and absence through illness or hospitalization will more frequently interrupt the slow educational progress.

In the above situation it will not be possible to balance work with seriously handicapped pupils by work with those less handicapped with near-normal educational progress, for the latter group will not be in the school. Against this, the need to develop new methods through experimental teaching will attract some teachers and for them provide a balance. Others may derive personal satisfaction from the challenge presented by the children, or from the commitment required for work with seriously handicapped pupils, to a degree which balances the slow gradient of educational progress by the children. As parents of children with serious disabilities are usually closely involved with schools, some teachers may derive satisfaction from the closer interaction with families which is made possible and so balance the constraints. If the broader concept of special educational needs prevails some special schools may admit a wider range of disabilities than at present so that some variety in the teachers' work may come from working in different areas of the school rather than at different levels. Many teachers who work with children who combine extremes of mental and physical disability perceive physical and personality differences in their pupils which are not obvious to visitors and thus they enjoy a variety and richness in the child group that is denied to outsiders. This may operate more widely in the special schools of the future.

Serious questions arise from the above considerations. Will sufficient teachers be motivated to remain in the special schools of the future? or will there be a tendency to desert them for the nearer normal educational satisfactions to be had in designated classes or resource centres? Will teachers remaining in the special schools lose contact with educational expectations? Will the motivation which keeps them there be sufficient to maintain educational initiative against the weight of care and medicine? Is it a 'good' thing, in terms of both professional and personal well-being, that a teacher should remain for long periods in a situation of severe disability and extremely slow or deviant educational progress? At present there can be no certain answers to these questions, which can only be resolved on the basis of experience. Some attempt is necessary, therefore, to guard against the dangers of extreme separation from the mainstream of education.

The movement of all special education into ordinary schools would resolve one major problem of separation for good. However, though not to be abandoned as an objective, it cannot be accepted as a short- or medium-term solution and the problem of separation must be approached through planned special–ordinary school interaction.

Special–Ordinary School Interaction

A radical approach to ordinary and special school interaction must break down the present isolation of special schools in the system in a way that will override the greater 'distance' which may develop in the future and at the same time prevent the isolation of special school teachers from their colleagues in designated classes, resource centres and on the general staff of ordinary schools. It should also create a situation in which teachers working with severely hand-icapped pupils in the special schools find it easier than at present to maintain contact with mainstream education through balance and variety in their teaching experience. To achieve the objective it may be necessary to abandon current ideas about the staffing of special schools and think instead of staffing special education. Each designated unit or resource centre in an ordinary school should be closely associated with an appropriate special school. Normally there would be a trinity of primary unit, secondary unit and special school. The staffing of the units should be handled in the special education section of the LEA in the same manner as the staffing of the special school and the head of that school should have a special relationship with the units. All staff of special schools and designated units should be regarded as special education branch staff and teachers should be able to interchange between the three situations without any obstacles in relation to scale posts which they may hold. It would be advisable to have a single special education adviser or inspector responsible for the group of school and units in order to control and regulate staff interaction. There would also be a need to involve the headteachers of the host ordinary schools, for their schools would be affected by special education interchange and they should clear any arrangements before they operate. Meetings between the heads and teachers of the three school/units should be held from time to time to exchange ideas and discuss common problems while the host school inspectors and the special education inspectors might participate in some of the meetings. These arrangements would ensure adequate discussion of policy at school level and create valuable insight in top management. Staff interaction between special school and units would be by mutual agreement which also took account of the effects on pupils. But it would be necessary to establish that the interaction was a condition of the employment of teachers. The interaction between special school and units should also relate to interaction between the units and their host schools. Thus teachers from the special school, while working on the staff of a unit, would also participate in some teaching in the ordinary classes of the host school. Much thought and experiment would be required to develop this or a similar system of interchange but, properly developed, it could rid the system of isolation and bring special education as fully as possible into the mainstream of education. For the teachers, it would resolve many of the problems of balanced experience noted above to the extent that, in a few years time, a teacher aspiring to senior responsibility in special education could be expected to have experience of teaching in special schools and designated situations and to have kept a continuing contact with mainstream teaching.

Boarding special schools will present particular problems in the development of interaction similar to that outlined above. It may be that the need to place children away from home may overlap other educational needs so that the population of residential schools will be less concentrated at the extreme of disability. But the overall need to promote interaction and reduce the isolation of teachers will remain. Where boarding schools are within the area of the LEA then interaction with local day schools should not present too much difficulty. But where a boarding school is in the area of another LEA the situation becomes more complicated and calls for good cooperation between the LEAs and their schools. In this situation there will be advantages in the boarding school providing day places for local pupils who require special school placement. Here again, good cooperation is necessary and has the advantage of making maximum use of existing resources. Considerations such as these should form part of regional planning in special education.

The problem of the relationship between the remaining special schools and the mainstream system requires continuing careful thought and must be closely watched as the new system develops. Many of the suggestions made in the Warnock Report are fine so long as the special schools remain as they are now. But the committee appears to have paid too little attention to the effect on special schools of their suggestions for the movement of special education into ordinary schools. In teaching methods, curriculum, pace of learning, balance of education against care and post-school prospects for the pupils the difference between ordinary and special schools may be qualitative rather than quantitative. Consequently the sharing of resources and teaching *by the pupils*; the development of common aspects of curriculum; and short-term provision for pupils on the roll of ordinary schools may present more problems than have been anticipated. If the move to ordinary schools is successfully completed, even social interaction between pupils may need careful preparation and organization. A simple example highlights the situation. Once a designated unit is operating in an ordinary school, what is the point of pupils visiting from a special school to participate in part of the ordinary school curriculum? Surely in most cases of this kind such pupils would be better placed in the designated unit. Only the fact that a suitable designated unit was not available could justify the initial arrangement. If the point made in this paragraph appears exaggerated, consider the conditions for placement in a special school identified in the Warnock Report (DES 1978, p. 123):

1. Children with severe or complex physical, sensory or intellectual disabilities who require special facilities, teaching methods or expertise that it would be impracticable to provide in ordinary schools.
2. Children with severe emotional or behavioural disorders who have very great difficulty in forming relationships with others or whose behaviour is so extreme or unpredictable that it causes severe disruption in an ordinary school or inhibits the educational progress of other children.
3. Children with less severe disabilities, often in combination, who despite special help do not perform well in an ordinary school and are more likely to thrive in the more intimate communal and educational setting of a special school.

Note, too, that when places in designated units are widely available only the extremes of the above groups will be in special schools. This is not an argument against the movement of as much special education as possible into properly-designated situations in ordinary schools. It is, rather, a case for a much more careful and realistic look at what the move implies for the remaining special schools.

The School Curriculum

This is not the place for a detailed discussion of the development of curricula in special education, for that would require a book in itself. It is necessary, however, to identify problems and indicate broadly the direction in which schools should advance. The Warnock Report identified certain weaknesses: a preoccupation with teaching methods at the expense of consideration of objectives, materials or learning experiences; inadequate attention to experiences relating to post-school life; too little attention to planned programmes and their effectiveness. Evidence suggested that special schools underestimated the ability of pupils at all levels and considered that the curricula should be broadened in many directions (DES 1978, para. 11.8). The committee found evidence to substantiate these points but they also found schools providing excellent curricula (DES 1978, para. 11.13). The situation is clear. Excellent special schools exist but are a minority in the system, so the problem is that of bringing all schools nearer to the level of the best. Wherever curriculum quality was high two main factors emerged: well-defined guidelines for each area of the curriculum; and programmes for individual children with well-defined, short-term goals within a general plan. Other marks of quality were continuity of approach, consistency among staff, agreed goals, and close work with the supporting services.

To improve curricula in the special schools and other situations which will provide special education it is essential that planning should start with the children and their needs and a knowledge of their home and neighbourhood circumstance, and consider the demands that may face the pupils as young adults. Objectives should be selected which cover emotional, social, intellectual and physical development and learning. They must be practicable and realistically related to the children for whom they are intended with the steps by which they are to be attained carefully worked out; and there must be an organized means of judging whether or not the objectives have been attained. Clear knowledge of objectives and an intimate knowledge of the pupils will shape the choice of experiences, materials and teaching and learning methods to be utilized by the teacher in her work. The whole of the curriculum process and content will require regular and continuing review if high quality is to be achieved and maintained. Much work will be required in curriculum development, and for children with special educational needs most of it must be school-based so that development and implementation go hand in hand.

Since the principles of curriculum for special needs were summarized in the Warnock Report a new technique for curriculum control and development has become available in schools—microelectronics and information technology. Its growth is typified in the Special Education Microelectronics Resource Centres (SEMERCs).[2] The centres have stimulated thought, experiment and practice in a rapidly growing field, though the technique has still to attain its full impact in the schools. Used only in terms of teaching material organization and individual records a micro-computer facilitates a control not previously available and brings within manageable limits the individualization of curriculum, teaching and timetables necessary if the special needs resource centre is to be fully effective. A recent publication summarized the extent and possibilities for wider curriculum applications (Brennan 1985), while the section headings from another illustrate possibilities in a pertinent manner: 'Improving self-esteem and motivation'; 'Improving language skills'; 'Improving reading, writing and spelling'; 'Improving number skills'; 'Improving problem solving strategies'; 'Changing the curriculum' (Hope 1986; see also Hogg 1984).

As with all new techniques, time and experience are required in order fully to exploit possibilities, and the early moves in this field were marked by repetitive programmes only marginally stimulating, emphasis on behavioural programmes, and a tendency for children to work at the computer in isolation. These are now changing, as is illustrated above. It has also been suggested that teachers will be safeguarded from the initial errors provided that they:

(a) use the techniques to link children and foster intercommunication;
(b) relate microelectronics to other traditional classroom methods;
(c) link the techniques to real classroom investigations;
(d) let lesson objectives control the interaction of pupils; and
(e) make sure reinforcement by the hardware is also reinforced by the teacher (McCall 1986).

The work involved in curriculum development is rarely allowed for when the staffing levels of schools are considered; it may become necessary to do so, not only for special schools but also for designated classes and resource centres. Special attention will have to be given to the problems faced by children with special needs when they leave school, to vocational guidance, career and consumer education and to health education in all its aspects. This part of curriculum requires a firm, practical base in real experience outside the school.

A new dimension has been introduced in many schools through the Technical & Vocational Education Initiative 14–16, a partnership between the DES, LEAs and Manpower Services Commission which seeks to relate education to life and work skills, marry general and vocational education, and has objectives that are not wholly dissimilar to those outlined in the last paragraph. Projects in TVEI aspire to cover the whole range of ability but at the lowest level (no graded CSE results) the take-up in projects, at 4 per cent, is only about half the proportion at that level in the 1983–4 year group (MSC 1985). However, in the criteria for projects, consideration to accommodating some students with special educational needs is identified and it is claimed that such students are participating in about half of the projects, where ever possible supported by specialist staff and integrated into the mainstream of provision. There are some non-integrated projects with special educational needs participation (MSC 1985):

(a)   where a special unit is attached to a project school;
(b)   where a special school is a member of a project consortium;
(c)   where there are arrangements for a special school to have access to a project.

Pupils with behavioural problems from an ordinary school unit and others with severe learning difficulties from a special school are among those participating in projects within the above arrangements in Scotland, Cumbria and the West Midlands. In its next phase of development TVEI is to extend into the 16–19 age range where it should widen the possibility of sixth-form work for pupils with special educational needs.

Further Education

Further education is an area almost totally unexplored for young people with special needs. Its problems are relatively uncharted and this is surely partly responsible for the unemployment and underemployment of handicapped young people. Naturally, education for the 16–19 age group must face the fact that for many of those with special needs, the objectives of further education must include many which normal pupils have achieved during the years of statutory education. Moreover, there is a direct relationship between what can actually be achieved in further education and the quality of the curriculum which the students have previously followed.

Pupils with special educational needs on the roll of a school have the right to continue in education up to age 19, though this does not seem to be widely known. Nevertheless there is some increase in the 16+ take-up mainly by pupils following mainstream curriculum with support or those with mental disabilities following developmental curricula. In future ordinary schools should have a major role in 16–19 education. The development of special units in ordinary schools, or better, special needs resource centres, should stimulate the provision of courses suitable for a range of pupils with special needs in both academic and practical fields and it should be made possible for pupils from special schools to join the courses. Three trends should assist the developments: first the social and life skills work already in hand; second the stimulus of TVEI projects; and third, the practical emphasis of the GCSE when introduced.

Not all young people wish to stay on in school and many exercise the option of taking courses in a College of Further Education. Young people with special needs should have the same option and, as the Warnock Report recognized, for many of them a FE college would be the most appropriate setting for their continued education (DES 1978, pp. 172–6). While the need is recognized suitable college provision has been slow to develop, haphazard, and unevenly distributed among different kinds of disability (FEU 1981; NUT 1982; Bradley and Hegarty 1982; see also Brennan 1985, pp. 160–8). Yet there has been much stimulating discussion about further education and special needs, particularly in terms of curriculum content and development. The outcome is available in publications of the Further Education Curriculum Development Unit.[3] The work is of high quality and should stimulate anyone interested or involved in 16–19 education for young people with special needs. In terms of practical achievements it is now clear that FE colleges are able to provide courses adapted to the social and vocational needs of pupils with disabilities as well as developmental courses for those who require time to reach maturity. There should be some continuity between school and college as at every other critical transfer point in education and cooperation here is associated with successful courses. There also seems to be positive advantage in the involvement of both special needs and further education advisers in the planning and monitoring of courses. Joint conferences involving school and college staffs teaching young people with special needs have been reported as of great value by both groups and this sharing of experience has a great deal to offer that is of benefit to students.

Another development in the 16–19 age range is the Youth Training Scheme of the Manpower Services Commission (YTS 1986). The YTS schemes provide two years' vocational training with the aim of producing better-qualified young entrants to the labour market. There are special arrangements through a premium places system for young people with special educational needs who may enter training up to 21 years of age. To qualify, applicants must come within a special definition of disabled young person. Those classed as such:

(a) suffer from a physical, mental or sensory handicap, and/or
(b) have moderate or severe learning difficulties which put them at a substantial disadvantage in the labour market;
(c) are between 16 and 21 years of age;
(d) are endorsed by their careers office for entry to a premium place;
(e) are supported by a specialist careers officer or Disablement Resettlement Officer if in need of assistance or funding for special training needs.

Though the YTS is open to all young people regardless of disability, it is a condition that they are considered capable of eventually obtaining open employment. But the scheme does provide special help where appropriate in four main forms:

(a) Special aids to employment: oracle devices,[4] telephone amplifiers, etc.; essential aids. The recipient must be registered as disabled.
(b) Adaptations to premises or equipment: assistance towards ramps, chair-lifts, wide doors, etc.; 100 per cent grants up to a maximum of £6,000.
(c) Personal reader service for the blind: assistance towards the cost of a reader to help with induction and off-the-job training periods.
(d) Interpreter service for the deaf: assistance towards the cost of an interpreter to help with induction and off-the-job training.

The main MSC policy is that trainees should, whenever possible, be integrated into mainstream provision but positive action may be used where any disability group is underrepresented in any skill or occupation. This allows a situation to be created in which the disabled persons are able to train appropriately for eventual open participation in the skill area or occupation.

A special aspect of further education concerns young people with severe learning difficulties. There are various interactions between schools and colleges—some involve part-time attendance at college from school, others from the adult centre; college tutors contribute in some centres; joint appointments between special and further education stimulate interaction; and there are permanent schemes where young people move from school to a course in a FE college before entering the adult centre. More common is the appointment of teachers to work with young entrants to the centres and this represents a genuine attempt to continue their education.

Of the situations observed the school-college-centre arrangement seemed the most suitable. Continuity of learning on from school was good; the school curriculum was improved by the removal of activities more suited to the college phase; the time and effort saved contributed to improved quality of learning in school; the broadening effect of college showed clearly in the growing maturity of the handicapped young people; and they entered the adult centre much more 'adult' in the sense of the older population to be found there. Within the centre the new arrangement had an advantage in narrowing the problems facing the staff and allowing them to concentrate on more 'adult' activities. A nationwide and permanent arrangement of the kind described could bring qualitative changes in the continued education of young people with severe learning difficulties.[5]

Adult education

In discussing the needs of mentally handicapped young people above, we have been thinking of developmental continued education that takes up and furthers what has been achieved through the school curriculum. The need here is not for continuous developmental curricula but for leisure and cultural activities which capture the interests of the adults and give some pattern and purpose to their lives. This contribution is more appropriate for adult education, and where this is organized separately from further education the contribution would be more suited to the organization of an Adult Education Institute. The institutes could also develop another contribution to special education. It will be recalled that in considering pre-school education parent education was accorded considerable importance in the work of the home teacher. Her work could be supported by adult education courses designed for parents of handicapped children. Other general courses might attempt to disseminate knowledge of handicap and the place of handicapped people in society at the level of popular information with the objective of contributing to the improvement of community attitudes to disabled members. Adult education could also do more to inform handicapped persons and their families about the support that is available from public sources and voluntary bodies and the manner in which the support may be secured. There is also the problem of hospitalized and home-bound adults. During their school years the hospital schools or groups and the home tuition service provide for children with these special educational needs but the situation of adults is not so clearly covered. There is reason to believe that many adults in the above situation are under-occupied, lack intellectual or cultural activities and may be downright lonely. Many voluntary bodies do what they can, often with financial support from public funds. But there is a case for more serious consideration of the role of the education service and, if developed, it would be an appropriate task for special adult education.

Summary

Pre-school education is seen as a growth area of special needs involving home teachers and parents who are the first educators. For children in school early detection and intervention are imperatives requiring a combination of annual surveys and continuous structured classroom observation. Most children found to require special education will receive it as an arrangement within their own school, but others may require formal assessment by the LEA. Where considered necessary the LEA will determine their special educational needs through a 'statement' though, wherever possible, they should be educated in an ordinary school. It is suggested that a resource centre for special needs is required in every large secondary or primary school, though where this is not possible other arrangements such as neighbourhood placements may be required. An advisory and support service for special needs is seen as essential in each LEA.

Special schools will continue to be required as ordinary school provision is developed. But as it expands, and teachers become more experienced there will be reduced reliance on special school support. The population of special schools will also change, with children showing more serious or complex needs. There may be increased danger of separation from mainstream education; the curriculum, too, will require development.

In all schools there is need to expand 16–19 education for pupils with special educational needs, through suitable sixth-form courses or involvement in TVEI projects.[6] Some pupils will choose to move to Colleges of Further Education where suitable courses should also be developed and there should be wider participation in suitable YTS projects.[7] Further Education courses for students with severe learning difficulties should be available to all, intervening between school and the senior training centre.

Adult education requires expansion to meet the needs of mentally and physically handicapped people in day centres. And adult classes could assist the parents of handicapped children to understand their child's needs. By providing suitable courses in the community adult education could contribute to changing people's attitudes to disability in a manner necessary if there is to be full educational and social integration in society. Education for home-bound adults is seen as an area for development.

Notes

1. For an example, see ILEA (1986, p. 240); and the ILEA Learning Resource Centre's *Classroom Observation Procedures File*.
2. SEMERCs are for teachers who wish to explore the use of microelectronics and information technology in their work with children with special educational needs. There are four centres and the National Co-ordinator is Mary Hope, Council for Educational Technology, 3 Devonshire Street, London W1N 2BA. The centres disseminate information, participate in teacher training, stimulate curriculum development and demonstrate equipment. Of special interest is *Briefing*, a series of pertinent information sheets available from Mary Hope or the SEMERCs.
3. Further Education Curriculum Review and Development Unit (FEU), Elizabeth House, York Road, London SE1 7PH; Publications Despatch Centre, DES, Honeypot Lane, Canons Park, Middlesex HA7 1AZ. Later publications from: Lengman/FEU Publications, Longman Resources Unit, 62 Hallfield Road, Layerthorpe, York YO3 7XQ. See especially: *A College Guide: Meeting Special Educational Needs*.
4. Oracle devices. A range of cummunication equipment. Loop systems for the deaf, voice box activators for severely physically handicapped; VTU units for deaf to deaf communications, through visual stations etc.
5. In the spring of 1986 the TVEI unit of the MSC held a conference with the Bureau for Handicapped Students to consider TVEI and special educational needs. A publication based on the conference is due for publication in the autumn of 1986.
6. *TVEI Insight* is available free from the MSC Distribution Unit (Dept TVEI), Room E825, Moorfoot, Sheffield S1 4PQ. Issue no. 4, December 1985, carries an article on the involvement in a TVEI project of pupils with severe learning difficulties. A booklet on this involvement (Lilybank Booklet) is available from John Travers, TVEI, James Watt College, Finnart Street, Greenock, Renfrewshire.
7. The CET/FE project on 'The Use of Information Technology with Students with Special Needs in Further Education' began in 1985 and terminates in 1987. Ten FE colleges are involved in work with students with moderate learning difficulties using aspects of CPVE Core Areas: communications; social skills and problem-solving; numeracy; creative, personal and career development. Information is available from Mary Hope (see note 2) or P. Fowler, 285 Buxton Road, Macclesfield, Cheshire SK11 7ET (0625 25062), enclosing an A4 stamped self-addressed envelope.

References

Boxall, M. (1976), *Nurture Groups in Primary Schools*, ILEA.
Bradley, J. and Hegarty S. (1982), *Stretching the System*, FEU.
Brennan, W. K. (1985), *Curriculum for Special Needs*, Open University Press.
Department of Education and Science (1978), *Special Educational Needs* (Warnock Report), Cmnd. 7212, HMSO.

Further Education Curriculum Development Unit (1981), *Students with Special Needs in Further Education*, FEU.

Hogg, B. (1984), *Microelectronics and Special Educational Needs*, National Council for Special Education.

Hope, M. (1986), *The Magic of the Micro: a Resource for Children with Learning Difficulties*, Council for Educational Texchnology.

Inner London Education Authority (1986), *Educational Opportunities for All* (Fish Report), ILEA.

McCall, C. (1986), 'Postscript' in Hope (1986).

Manpower Services Commission (1985), *TVEI Review*, MSC.

National Union of Teachers (1982), *Survey of Educational Provision for 16–19-year-olds with Special Educational Needs*, NUT.

Youth Training Scheme (1986), *Training for Skills*, MSC.

CHAPTER 6

Changing Special Education

Where Are We Now?

The early chapters of this book attempted to show the kind of changes which have taken place in special education. Extension of the legally-defined categories of handicapped children failed to generate the flexibility in schools which was recognized as necessary by their parents and by teachers and this remained true even when a degree of informality was introduced into the system. Associated with this was growing dissatisfaction with the medical model which prevailed in special education. Disability of mind or body; treatment as a concept dominating a developmental, educational process; and a system of assessment for special education heavily influenced by professionals neither engaged in nor experienced in the teaching and education of the children being assessed; these factors also contributed to dissatisfaction. The response was a combined pressure for multidisciplinary approaches to assessment with the emphasis on education and a system based upon a description of the special educational needs of children to which could be related the proposals for their education. Other factors were also at work. The importance of the first years of a child's life was clearly demonstrated and with it the unique position of the parents as educators in those years, as well as the value of good quality pre-school education. Meanwhile a new democracy was abroad which emphasized the rights of individuals to information and it was reflected in the parent movement, in particular in the rights of the parents of children with disabilities not only to be informed, but to be consulted and fully involved in any assessment of their child's needs and proposals for the child's special education. As segregation in secondary education has generally faded with the growth of comprehensive secondary schools, so the pressure increased for the education of more children with disabilities within the ordinary schools in preference to education in the separate special schools. At the same time, it was noted, the greater part of public expenditure on special education found its outlet in the expansion of special school provision which absorbed most of the output of teachers specially trained to work with children with special needs. The opportunities afforded by legislation for the education of handicapped children in ordinary schools were not exploited. And, perhaps even more important, where good provision existed in ordinary schools it more often resulted from the initiative of the teachers concerned than from positive and purposeful planning by the local education authorities. By the end of the 1970s there were still pupils waiting for places in the special schools considered necessary for their education. But far greater in number, and not necessarily less at risk, were the children in ordinary schools with learning, behavioural or other difficulties for whom no adequate special teaching was provided. Ironically, though thin on the ground, the good situations noted above were adequate demonstration that the needs of most of these children could be appropriately and efficiently provided for within ordinary schools. Through all this there was increasing questioning of the education offered in schools, particularly in terms of the basic knowledge and life skills required for participation in society as adult members and workers. Special education was not exempt from this, and, inevitably, the weight fell on the special schools. It was realized that many children with special needs, because of the operation of those needs, could not be expected to achieve the normal goals of school leavers within the years of statutory education. The response was a demand for better provision for children with special needs in further education—an area found to be almost wholly unexploited so far as the needs of these young people were concerned.

The Warnock Report

The culmination of the above pressures and changes saw the appointment of the Warnock Committee to which constant reference has been made. In presenting their report the committee projected development in special education over a twenty-year time span and this should be kept in mind when assessing progress towards implimentation. To guide action, however, three areas of first priority were identified (DES 1978, pp. 336–7):

1.   Provision for children under 5 with special educational needs. This was to include the recognition and involvement of parents as

the first educators of their children; substantial expansion of nursery education for all children; extension of peripatetic teaching services to all types of disability in young children; provision of professional help and advice from supporting services, including the proposed special education advisory and support service, to playgroups, opportunity groups, day nurseries and, above all, parents.

2.   Provision for young people over 16 with special educational needs. This included: more opportunity to continue education at school or in further education and to receive careers guidance; variety of provision in ordinary courses and special courses with a special Further Education unit in each region; a specifically educational element in adult training centres and day centres; and necessary financial support to enable young people with special needs to undertake courses of further and higher education.

3.   Teacher training should include: a special education element in all courses of initial teacher training, short courses of one week (or equivalent) duration on special educational needs to be taken by the great majority of serving teachers within a few years; one year full-time (or equivalent) courses leading to a qualification in special education for teachers with a defined responsibility for children with special educational needs; other short courses on different aspects of special education; and the promotion of research and development to increase knowledge and understanding of different aspects of special education.

In addition, among over 200 recommendations, the report recommended changes in assessment procedures leading to a statement of special educational need, a clear definition of the circumstances identifying special education, and described the variety of special educational situations necessary to meet them. It recommended the appointment of a 'named person' for all children with special educational needs. The remit of the committee covered England, Scotland and Wales with the report submitted to the Secretary of State for Education and Science; the Secretary of State for Scotland; and the Secretary of State for Wales.

The Education Act 1981 (Special Educational Needs

The Education Act 1981 establishes that a child has a special educational need if he or she has a learning difficulty significantly greater than the majority of children of the same age or a disability which prevents the use of educational facilities of a kind generally provided in the schools for children of that age. Special educational provision is educational provision which is additional to, or otherwise different   from,   the   educational   provision   made   generally for children the same age as the child concerned in schools maintained by the LEA. It is the duty of the LEA to identify and assess children over 2 years of age in their area who may have special educational needs. In doing this they must seek medical, psychological and educational advice. Where it decides it is necessary, the LEA must determine the special education to be provided by making a statement of special educational needs which must also set out the proposals for meeting them. Parents dissatisfied with the LEA decision may appeal, first to the local appeal committee then, if necessary, to the Secretary of State. Where the LEA does *not* make a statement after assessment, dissatisfied parents may appeal to the Secretary of State. Requests from parents for the assessment of their children must be granted by the LEA unless they are unreasonable. It is also the duty of the LEA to inform parents of the intention to assess their child's needs, to name an officer who will give them further information, and to make sure that they know of their rights to present evidence to the assessment and, if necessary, appeal against its outcome. A 'named person' will be appointed to support the parents of children for whom the LEA has made a statement of special educational needs.

The LEA has a duty to educate in ordinary schools those children for whom it has made a statement providing that appropriate special education is available compatible with the efficient education of other children and the efficient use of resources and that the views of parents have been considered. Headteachers and governors of ordinary schools have a duty to ensure that children with special educational needs participate in school activities with pupils without such needs, that the teachers who teach them are aware of their needs; and that all teachers are aware of the importance of identifying and providing for such pupils. The LEA must keep its arrangements for special education under review and the needs of pupils for whom the authority has made a statement must be reviewed annually.

Special schools are to continue and the Secretary of State has made regulations defining conditions for recognition of a special school. Similar regulations define conditions for the recognition of independent schools as special schools. Only schools meeting the conditions and approved by the Secretary of State may be used by LEAs for the placement of children with special educational needs. LEAs wishing to close special schools must give notice to parents of children, other LEAs with children in the school and any interested bodies. The proposal and any objections must go to the Secretary of State whose approval is necessary before the LEA may cease to maintain the school. Though the Education Act 1981 applies only to England and Wales, legislation in Scotland and for Northern Ireland has created similar rights for pupils with special educational needs and their parents (See Appendix 8).

A Comparison

To what extent does the legislation in the Education Act 1981 incorporate the recommendations made in the Warnock Report, about which members of the committee were unanimous and which was widely welcomed by professionals in special education and the parents of children with special educational needs? A short answer is: to a very limited extent. An editorial in the journal *Special Education* (vol. 8, no. 1, March 1981) puts the point well:

> The bill has been described by Mr Niel Kinnock as 'a Michelin guide to nowhere'. Perhaps it would be fairer to say, as he did in the same second reading debate in the Commons on February 2, that, like Brighton pier, 'it is good as far as it goes but it is not much of a way to get to France'. If, for France, are substituted the Warnock Report's three priority areas of provision for the under fives, the over 16s and teacher training, plus more watertight safeguards about the quality of special education provision in ordinary schools, the description is apt.

There is nothing in the Act which will increase pressure for extended and improved special education in the pre-school years, though the right of the LEA to operate there is made somewhat clearer, while further education and teacher training receive no attention. The failure to establish any minimum standards for the provision of special education in ordinary schools contrasts markedly with the stated intention to establish conditions to regulate both LEA special schools and independent schools intending to admit children with special needs. The contrast is marked because it appears in an Act one intention of which is that more special education should be provided within ordinary schools. Some critics of the act relate the limitations to the absence of additional resources for implementation, while others see that as the reason for the vague definitions of special educational need and special education.

Adoption of the definitions recommended in the Warnock Report (see Chapter 4) would have related the definitions to resources and teachers and probably could not be contemplated in view of the decision on resources. Unfortunately the vagueness will have other effects. The definitions in the Act relate a child's needs to the generality of others of the same age in the locality and the same is true of definitions of special education provision. Nothing is as effective as generalization for promoting irresolvable argument, so it may be that the Act will generate misunderstanding between parents and LEAs. But more important, the approach abandons any attempt by central government to secure equality of special educational opportunity throughout the different regions of England and Wales. Similarly, the Act lacks any indication of an understanding of the close cooperation between the public services which has been shown to be necessary if special education is to be extended into ordinary schools and improved in quality both there and in special schools, though a subsequent circular did something to rectify the omission (DES 1983). And there is no concept of the immense task which faces initial and in-service training if properly-prepared teachers are to be available for both tasks with adequate support from experienced Advisory and Support Services in special education.

In contrast to the above, apologists for the Act regard the limitations as a realistic acceptance of the prevailing economic difficulties preventing the allocation of additional resources. They also point to the many recommendations of the Warnock Report that could be implemented without additional resources and, indeed, without legislation. Supporters also emphasize the positive aspects of the Act: the abolition of categories, the concept of special need, the definition of LEA responsibilities, the identification of parental rights and the requirement for integration.

Integration

The education of children with special educational needs in ordinary schools and classes has become *the* issue of the 1980s mainly as a result of the Warnock Report and the Education Act 1981. It is usually overlooked that both these sources favour the continuation of special schools as necessary for some children with special needs. The main teachers' associations follow a similar line, supporting integration but alongside the retention of special schools. Parents and the community at large also give general support to provision within ordinary schools but usually support the retention of special schools, as LEAs soon discover from the protests against proposed closures. What the pupils think is more difficult to ascertain as they are rarely asked for their opinion. An exception is a survey of over 300 secondary age pupils in special schools, conducted by the ILEA Research and Statistics Branch. Like parents and the community, the pupils had divided opinions. Few supported integration for all pupils with special educational needs. Most support came from pupils in schools for emotional and behavioural difficulties or motor impairment; in schools for delicate or deaf pupils there was no support for integration for all.

Expressing a personal choice, most pupils at schools for EBD and motor impairment opted for mainstream placement; visually impaired pupils were divided in their choice; and most delicate and deaf pupils chose the special school or unit. The survey did not include pupils who were autistic or had severe learning difficulties (*Times Educational Supplement* 1986). A survey of NUT members in ILEA shows considerable accord with the views of pupils. Respondents favoured provision in ordinary schools (though with increased resources) and the continuation of special schools in a comprehensive system (Special Children 1986). Two things should be noted about this consensus: first, it does not represent a qualitative change, for the same could be said of any period since the 1944 Education Act, as was shown in Chapter 3; and second, it suggests a general lack of confidence in the ability of ordinary schools to meet the full range of special needs.

That there are reservations about full integration should surprise no one. Ordinary schools and the teachers in them have been subject to criticism for a decade or more. Schools are deprived of resources; what they have are used ineffectively; curriculum is inadequate and out of touch with the times; teacher morale is at a low ebb; one-third of lessons taught are less than satisfactory; provision for children with special needs is haphazard and ineffective; and teachers given the responsibility are often inexperienced: this is the message of the media, usually based upon HMI reports or statements by teachers' representatives, with reinforcement from politicians and Secretaries of State. Further, parents and others are confused by the wide variation among LEAs in their response to the 1981 Act. Even adjacent LEAs may have different policies on the making of statements of special need, on the degree of parental involvement, on what they mean by 'integration', or on the future role of special schools (Saunders and Stafford 1986; Pearson and Lindsay 1986; Rogers 1986). Nor is it surprising, in these circumstances, that the movement of children with special needs into ordinary schools has been minimal as shown by the data in Chapter 1. Perhaps the LEAs themselves lack confidence!

In the current situation it is not necessarily wrong to proceed with caution: how could it be when every move, however sound theoretically, may put at risk children with special needs. But that is not an excuse for inactivity. Advance on a wide front may not be possible but wherever individual situations are suitable resources should be concentrated to set up pilot schemes for integration. In this way administrative and teaching experience will be accumulated and the real possibilities of integration demonstrated to the doubters. Successful ventures should be objectively evaluated and the information disseminated using the wider media in order to generate public confidence. The objective should be to establish a range of verified educational situations that matches the range and severity of special needs. Special schools may initially form part of that range but it should include the special classes and support centres in ordinary schools that may eventually make special schools unnecessary. At the same time there must be awareness of the dangers of random development. What is learned must be incorporated and systematized for only a flexible *system* of special education will provide for all current needs and offer scope for meeting any that develop in the future.

Parents

If integration has become the issue of the 1980s then it is followed closely by that of parental rights in the assessment and education of children with special educational needs, part of the widening of participant democracy that seems to be part of the times. But it is quite clear that there is a wide gap between theoretical rights and what takes place in practice. Doubts are cast upon officials' concepts of parental aspirations, with suggestions that they are more radical than the reality (Sanders and Stafford 1986). It is claimed that many LEAs are unforthcoming in their provision of information for parents and that where it is forthcoming there is wide variation in the content and its manner of communication (Rogers 1986). At the same time less seems to be heard about the responsibilities of parents to cooperate with schools in the education of their children; to provide the consistency and regulation in the early years that is conducive to order, self-regulation and personal constraint in later years. Perhaps even here LEAs and the system of education are at fault. Does social education prepare young people for that adult role? Are we wanting people to participate in a democratic manner without ensuring that they acquire in their education the skills that make it possible? Are our administrators and teachers themselves in possession of the participation skills which *they* require if democracy is to function? And is dual ignorance the root of the trouble? The answer is not as simple as many people believe. If teachers and parents are to be partners then both have skills to learn and they will learn more effectively if they are made aware of it. This is not the political democracy of casting votes. It is the more subtle personal democracy that depends upon sensitivity to others, recognition of rights, ability and willingness to develop a synthesis from apparently opposed positions. One thing *is* certain: legislation alone will not achieve it.

To What Purpose?

In the present circumstances it is important that those concerned with special education—parents, teachers, supporting professionals, care workers, administrators, advisers and members of education authorities—should maintain a sense of purpose which goes beyond immediate short-term considerations. The children described in Chapter 1 are typical. In future others like them will have similar special needs and they, too, will require special education appropriate to their needs. But their special education should be more than appropriate: it should also be of good quality and it should be so as a result of planning with purpose rather than fortuitous circumstances. It cannot, at present, be confidently asserted that every child who needs it is receiving special education which reflects the above qualities, and indeed the education of some may lack all three. So there is no shortage of work to be done at all levels.

Achieving appropriateness and good quality as a result of planning is more important than the place in which the education is delivered. Nevertheless, the current ethos which demands that wherever possible children with special needs should be educated in ordinary schools and interact with children without such needs is correct and it is right that the principle should be encompassed in legislation. Experience has shown, however, that there is much which may 'slip away' between legislation and practice and this time it must not be allowed to happen. Nor should it be overlooked that among the most disadvantaged children in our schools are those in the ordinary schools who have special educational needs about which little is being done. Consequently, one of the first moves in ordinary schools should be to make proper arrangements for the education of pupils with special needs *who are already in the schools*. In no circumstances should the needs of such pupils be ignored in premature attempts to place in ordinary schools pupils with more severe special needs.

The Education Act 1981, notwithstanding its limitations, does allow a start to be made on implementing the broader concept of special education. It removes the concept of disabilities of mind or body, ends the idea of special educational treatment, and abolishes the legal categories of handicapped children. These are essential requirements, but of themselves they will not convert the concept of broader areas of special educational needs into the central feature of special education in action. For that changed attitudes are essential. Handicapped people must be seen as in full membership of the community, the notion of a 'dole' for the handicapped should disappear and be replaced by opportunities for them to contribute to society on the basis of their abilities, as all citizens should. The concept of equality, of treating people alike, should give way to the concept of equity, of treating people according to their needs. No longer should a single disability be regarded as an all-round handicap or an obtrusive one as a sign that the person has fewer emotional or social needs than others. Teachers in ordinary schools must lose their fear of children with special needs and those in special schools learn to admit that for some of their pupils the ordinary school might be a more appropriate place for their special education. Educationists, careers officer, and employers must seek new opportunities for young people in further education, in training and in employment. Parents of normal children must lose the fear that the presence of children with special needs in the school will be a disadvantage for their own children. Instead they should use their collective power to insist that the Local Education Authority makes facilities available to meet the needs of *all* children in the schools. These are the attitudes necessary to make a reality of the broader concept of special education and it is to the Warnock Report that parents and educators must look for their lead.

References

Department of Education and Science (1978), *Special Educational Needs* (Warnock Report), Cmnd. 7212, HMSO.

DES (1983), *Assessments and Statements of Special Educational Needs*, Circular 1/83 (Welsh Office Circular 21/83), HMSO.

Pearson, L. and Lindsay, G. (1986), *Special Needs in the Primary School: Identification and Intervention*, NFER-Nelson.

Rogers, R. (1986), *Caught in the Act*, CSIE/Spastics Society.

Saunders, S. A. and Stafford, P. (1986), 'Parental Perceptions and the 1981 Act', *British Journal of Special Education*, vol. 13, no. 1.

Special Children (1986) N°6 December 1986 p. 5.

Times Educational Supplement (1986), 'Handicapped Children Speak of Mainstream Fear', 28 November, p. 3. See also *Special Children* N°6 op. sit.

APPENDIX 1

Categories of Handicapped Pupils

The categories below are as set out in *Handicapped Pupils and Special Schools Regulations 1959*, as amended 1962. The figures in brackets indicate the maximum class sizes allowed until replaced by a recommended pupil–teacher ratio in 1973. First figure class size; second figure pupil–teacher ratio.

Blind pupils, that is to say, pupils who have no sight or whose sight is or is likely to become so defective that they require education by methods not involving the use of sight. (15; 1:6)

Partially sighted pupils, that is to say, pupils who by reason of defective vision cannot follow the normal regime of ordinary schools without detriment to their sight or to their educational development, but can be educated by special methods involving the use of sight. (15; 1:8.5)

Deaf pupils, that is to say, pupils with impaired hearing who require education by methods suitable for pupils with little or no naturally acquired speech or language. (10; 1:6.5 primary, 1:5.5 secondary)

Partially hearing pupils, that is to say, pupils with impaired hearing whose development of speech and language, even if retarded, is following a normal pattern, and who require for their education special arrangements or facilities though not necessarily all the educational methods used for deaf pupils. (10; 1:6.5 primary, 1:6.5 secondary)

Educationally subnormal pupils, that is to say, pupils who, by reason of limited ability or other conditions resulting in educational retardation, require some specialized form of education wholly or partly in substitution for the education normally given in ordinary schools. (20; ESN(S) 1:8.5, ESN(M) 1:11)

Epileptic pupils, that is to say, pupils who by reason of epilepsy cannot be educated under the normal regime of ordinary schools without detriment to themselves or other pupils. (20; 1:9)

Maladjusted pupils, that is to say, pupils who show evidence of emotional instability or psychological disturbance and require special educational treatment in order to effect their personal, social or educational readjustment. (15; 1:6)

Physically handicapped pupils, that is to say, pupils not suffering solely from a defect of sight or hearing who by reason of disease or crippling defect cannot, without detriment to their health or educational development, be satisfactorily educated under the normal regime of ordinary schools. (20; 1:7)

Pupils suffering from speech defect, that is to say, pupils who on account of defect or lack of speech not due to deafness require special educational treatment. (as per deaf pupils)

Delicate pupils, that is to say, pupils not falling under any other category in this regulation, who by reason of impaired physical condition need a change of environment or cannot, without risk to their health or educational development, be educated under the normal regime of ordinary schools. (30; 1:8)

Useful Addresses

Advisory Centre for Education, 18 Victoria Park Square, London E2 9PB.

Association of Professions for the Mentally Handicapped, 126 Albert Street, London NW1 7NF.

Association of Workers for Maladjusted Children, New Barnes School, Church Lane, Toddington, Glos. GL54 5DH.

British Association of Teachers of the Deaf, The Rycroft Centre, Stanley Road, Cheadle Hulme, Cheshire SK8 6RF.

British Dyslexia Association, 18 The Circus, Bath BA1 2ET.

British Epilepsy Association, 140 Holland Park Avenue, London W11 4UF.

Campaign for Advancement of State Education, Information from: Elizabeth Wallis, 25 Leybourne Park, Kew Gardens, Richmond, Surrey.

Centre on Environment for the Handicapped, 126 Albert Street, London NW1.

Centre for Studies on Integration in Education (CSIE), The Spastics Society, 16 Fitzroy Square, London WP1 5HQ.

Child Poverty Action Group, 1 Macklin Street, London WC2B 5NH.

Children's Legal Centre, 20 Crompton Terrace, London N1 2UN.

College of Teachers of the Blind, Royal School for the Blind, Church Road North, Wavertree, Liverpool L15 6TQ.

Confederation for the Advancement of State Education,
   England: 1 Windermere Avenue, Wembley, Middlesex HA9 8SH.
   Scotland: The Old Schoolhouse, Inverchaolain, Toward, Argyll.

Department of Education and Science (DES) (Special Education Division), York Road, London SE1 7PH.

Department of Health and Social Security (DHSS) (Child Health Branch), Alexander Fleming House, Elephant and Castle, London SE1 6BY.

Disabled Living Foundation, 346 Kensington High Street, London W14 8NS.

Home and School Council, 81 Rustlings Road, Sheffield S11 7AB.

Independent Panel of Special Education Experts, 20 Crompton Terrace, London N1 2UN.

Invalid Children's Aid Association, 126 Buckingham Palace Road, London SW1 9SB.

Manpower Services Commission, Moorfoot, Sheffield S1 4PQ (for TVEI and YTS).

National Association for the Education of the Partially Sighted, The East Anglian School, Church Road, Gt. Yarmouth NR31 6LP.

National Association for Mental Health, 22 Harley Street, London W1N 2ED.

National Association for Remedial Education, 77 Chignal Road, Chelmsford CM1 2JA.

National Association of Teachers of the Mentally Handicapped, 1 Beechfield Avenue, Urmstom, Manchester M31 3RT.

National Children's Bureau, 8 Wakley Street, London EC1V 7QE.

National Confederation of Parent–Teacher Associations, 43 Stonebridge Road, Northfleet, Gravesend, Kent.

National Council for Special Education, 1 Wood Street, Stratford-upon-Avon CV37 6JE.

National Foundation for Educational Research in England and Wales, The Mere, Upton Park, Slough, Berks SL1 2DQ.

National Deaf Children's Society, 31 Gloucester Place, London W1H 2EA.

National Elfrida Rathbone Society, 11a Whitworth Street, Manchester M1 3GW.

National Federation of Gateway Clubs, 17 Pembridge Square, London W2 4EP.

National Library for the Blind, Cromwell Road, Bredbury, Stockport SK6 2SG.

National Society for Autistic Children, 1a Golders Green Road, London NW11 8EA.

National Society for Mentally Handicapped Children, 17 Pembridge Square, London W2 4EP.

National Youth Bureau, 17–23 Albion Street, Leicester LE1 6GD.

Northern Ireland Council for Educational Research, 52 Malone Road, Belfast BT9 5BS.

Ombudsman (Commissioner for Local Administration),
  England: 21 Queen Anne's Gate, London SW1.
  Wales: Derwen House, Court Road, Bridgend, Glamorgan CF31 1BN.

Parliamentary Commissioner for Administration and Health Service, Church House, Great Smith Street, London SW1P 3BW.

Royal National Institute for the Blind, 224 Great Portland Street, London W1N 6AA.

Royal National Institute for the Deaf, 105 Gower Street, London WC1E 6AH.

The Schools Curriculum Development Unit, Newcombe House, 45 Notting Hill Gate, London W11 3JB.

Scottish Council for Research in Education, 16 Moray Place, Edinburgh EH3 6DR.

Scottish Council for Spastics, 22 Corstorphine Road, Edinburgh EH12 6HP.

Scottish Information Service for the Disabled, 18 Claremont Crescent, Edinburgh EH7 4QD.

Spastics Society, 12 Park Crescent, London W1N 4EQ.

Special Educational Needs Advisory Council, 271 Woolton Road, Liverpool L16 8NB.

Talking Books for the Handicapped, 49 Gt Cumberland Place, London W1H 7LH.

TVEI Unit, 236 Grays Inn Road, London WC1X 8HL.

Toy Libraries Association, Seabrook House, Wyllyotts Manor, Darkes Lane, Potters Bar, Herts EN6 2HL.

Volunary Council for Handicapped Children, 8 Wakley Street, London WC1V 7QE.

Local Information

Addresses may be found in the telephone directory:
    Social Services department of the local authority
    The Local Education Office
    Citizens Advice Bureau
    Local office of the Department of Health and Social Security

Statement of Special Educational Needs

I – Introduction

1.   In accordance with section 7 of the Education Act 1981 and the Education (Special Educational Needs) Regulations 1983, the following statement is made by the .... council ("the education authority") in respect of the child whose name and other participants are mentioned below.

Child

Surname..   Other names ....

Home address ....

....

....   Sex ....

Date of birth ....   Religion ....

Home language ....

Child's parent or guardian

Surname..   Other names ....

Home address ....   Relationship to child ....

....

....

2.   When assessing the child's special educational needs the education authority took into consideration, in accordance with Regulations 8 of the Regulations, the representations, evidence and advice set out in the Appendices to this statement.

II – Special educational needs

(Here, set out in accordance with section 7 of the 1981 Act, the child's special educational needs as assessed by the education authority.)

III – Special educational provision

(Here specify, in accordance with Regulation 10(1)(a), the special educational provision which the education authority consider appropriate to meet the needs specified in Part II.)

IV – Appropriate school or other arrangements

(Here specify, in accordance with Regulation 10(1)(b), the type of school and any particular school which the education authority consider appropriate for the child or the provision for his education otherwise than at a school which they consider appropriate.)

V – Additional non-educational provision

(Here specify, in accordance with Regulation 10(1)(c), any such additional provision as is there mentioned or record that there is no such additional provision.)

(Date)   (Signature of authenticating officer)

....

                                                             A duly authorised officer of the
                                                             education authority.

Appendices to the Statement of Special Educational Needs

Appendix A:Parental representations

(Here set out any written representations made by the parent of the child in pursuance of section 5(3)(d) of the Act and a summary which the parent has accepted as accurate of any oral representations so made or record that no such representations were made.)

Appendix B:Parental evidence

(Here set out any written evidence either submitted by the parent of the child in pursuance of section 5(3)(d) of the Act or submitted at his request or record that no such evidence was submitted.)

Appendix C:Educational advice

(Here set out the advice obtained in pursuance of Regulation 4(1)(a).)

Appendix D:Medical advice

(Here set out the advice obtained in pursuance of Regulation 4(1)(b).)

Appendix E:Psychological advice

(Here set out the advice obtained in pursuance of Regulation 4(1)(c).)

Appendix F:Other advice obtained by Education Authority

(Here set out any advice obtained in pursuance of Regulation 4(1)(d) or record that no such advice was sought.)

Appendix G:Information furnished by District Health Authority or Social Services Authority

(Here set out any such information as is mentioned in Regulation 8(d) or record that no such information was furnished.)

Note:

The above list follows the wording of the Education (Special Educational Needs) Regulations 1983. The educational, medical and psychological advice will be reproduced in Appendices C, D and E respectively. Appendices A, B, F and G will consist of copies of the relevant documents, or where none have been submitted, of a note to that effect.

Advice on Special Educational Needs: Suggested Checklist

(a) Description of the Child's Functioning

1. Description of the child's strengths and weaknesses

Physical State and Functioning
(physical health, developmental function, mobility, hearing, vision)

Emotional State
(link between stress, emotions and physical state)

Cognitive Functioning

Communication Skills
(verbal comprehension, expressive language, speech)

Perceptual and Motor Skills

Adaptive Skills

Social Skills and Interaction

Approaches and Attitudes to Learning

Educational Attainments

Self-image and Interests

Behaviour

2. Factors in the child's environment which lessen or contribute to his needs

In the Home and Family

At School

Elsewhere

3. Relevant aspects of the child's history

Personal

Medical

Educational

(b) Aims of Provision

1. General areas of development

Physical Development
(eg. to develop self-care skills)

Motor Development
(eg. to improve co-ordination of hand and fingers, to achieve hand—eye
co-ordination)

Cognitive Development
(eg. to develop the ability to classify)

Language Development
(eg. to improve expressive language skills)

Social Development
(eg. to stimulate social contact with peers)

2. Any specific areas of weakness or gaps in skills acquisition which impede the child's progress

Eg. short-term memory deficits

3. Suggested methods and approaches

Implications of the Child's Medical Condition
(eg. advice on the side-effects of medication for epilepsy)

Teaching and Learning Approaches
(eg. teaching methods for the blind or deaf, or teaching through other
specialised methods)

Emotional Climate and Social Regime
(eg. type of regime, size of class or school, need for individual attention)

(c) Facilities and Resources

1. Special Equipment

(eg. physical aids, auditory aids, visual aids)

2. Specialist Facilities

(eg. for incontinence, for medical examination, treatment and drug
administration)

3. Special Educational Resources

(eg. specialist equipment for teaching children with physical or sensory
disabilities, non-teaching aids)

4. Other Specialist Resources

(eg. Nursing, Social Work, Speech Therapy, Occupational Therapy,
Physiotherapy, Psychotherapy, Audiology, Orthoptics)

5. **Physical Environment**

    (eg. access and facilities for non-ambulant pupils, attention to lighting environment, attention to acoustic environment, attention to thermal environment, health care accommodation)

6. **School Organization and Attendance**

    (eg. day attendance, weekly boarding, termly boarding, relief hostel accommodation)

7. **Transport**

APPENDIX 5

Research Projects

Project Impact

This is a DES-funded project 1983–6, conducted jointly between the Hester Adrian Research Centre at the University of Manchester and Huddersfield Polytechnic. There are three parts to the research:

(a) The development and evaluation of a North-West Regional Modular Diploma—an advanced specialist qualification for teachers and others working with people with special needs.

(b) A follow-up of the EDY in-service package—a survey of all who received EDY diplomas in 1983; and a survey of all instructors known to have run courses.

(c) The development and evaluation of short school-focused courses in special educational needs.

See: J. Sebba, 'The Development and Evaluation of Short School-focused Courses on Special Educational Needs' *Educational and Child Psychology*, vol. 2, no. 3, 1985, pp. 130–7; and C. Robson, 'A Modular In-Service Advanced Qualification for Teachers of Children with Special Needs', *British Journal of In-Service Education*, vol. 11, no. 1, 1984, pp. 32–6.

Policy and Provision for Special Needs: The Implementation of the 1981 Education Act

This DES-funded project has investigated the response of LEAs in England to the 1981 Act, considering how it has influenced their policies and practices. Specific aims are identified as:

(a) the impact of the Act on those working in education, health and social services;

(b) the effectiveness of the Act is providing children access to provision appropriate to their special needs;

(c)   identification and description of practices in parental involvement, initial assessment, provision, review and reassessment;

(d)   the provision of information about alternative responses to the Act that will be of practical assistance to all those concerned with it.

The project is based in the University of London Institute of Education. News letters and interim papers have been produced and are available from Brian Goacher. See Special Children N°6 December 1986, p 7 Report of Dissemination Meeting.

Meeting Special Educational Needs—Support for the Ordinary School

Based at NFER during 1983–6, this DES funded project has the stated intention to be of substantial assistance to LEAs and schools in making the best sort of provision for children with special educational needs. It concentrates on:

(a)   allocation of resources and administrative support;

(b)   links between special and ordinary schools;

(c)   in-service training.

(d)   identifying and disseminating good practice.

1981 Education Act: Research, Dissemination and Management Project 1986–88.

This is a two year DES/DHSS funded project located jointly in London University Departments of Economic and Policy Studies in Education and Department of Child Development and Educational Psychology in association with The National Children's Bureau.

It is to focus on:

1. Strategic planning within and between authorities;

2. Administrative decisions about supporting, resourcing and determining the pattern of special needs in schools.

3. Decision making processes involved in 'statementing' procedures.

Examples of
LEA INSET Projects

Special Needs Action Programme (SNAP)

SNAP was developed in the city of Coventry out of a desire to use the experience resource of special education to support work with children with special educational needs in ordinary schools. There are three specific aims:

(a) to encourage and assist headteachers in developing procedures to identify pupils with special needs in their schools;
(b) to assist teachers to provide appropriate curriculum for such pupils;
(c) to coordinate special education services and facilities in support of teachers in ordinary schools.

There are four main areas in the programme:

(a) provision of information for headteachers and the coordinators appointed in each school;
(b) presentation of courses, first to coordinators and then as part of school-based staff development programmes;
(c) dissemination of materials that have been used and evaluated by experienced special education teachers;
(d) advice and help to schools by teachers and psychologist from a coordinated special education support service.

The approach has a high degree of structure with courses to be followed by co-ordinators and disseminators using specially prepared handbooks; it also develops a pyramid organization for the communication of information and knowledge. Practical activities are built into the procedures.

Examples of constituent courses are: Learning Difficulties, Daily Measurement, Hearing Difficulties, Visual Difficulties, Behaviour and Emotional Difficulties.

SNAP places emphasis on schools' taking responsibility for their own problems based upon the information acquired from the programme. The coordinator is a key person in this and schools are encouraged to appoint senior members of staff in the role.

Material developed in SNAP is now published by Drake Educational Associates Ltd. A useful reference is: M. Ainscow and J. Muncey, 'Learning Difficulties in the Primary School: An In-service Initiative', *Remedial Education*, vol. 18, no. 3, 1983, reprinted in C. J. Smith, ed., *New Directions in Remedial Education*, Falmer Press, 1985.

Special Needs Information Pack (SNIP)

This initiative comes from Essex LEA. The emphasis is on practical information and advice directly related to the classroom. Unlike SNAP, SNIP is designed for simultaneous use in the schools, as a reference tool and as a basis for school-initiated school-based in-service work. The stated aims are:

(a) to increase awareness about special educational needs in the ordinary school;

(b) to provide practical guidance and recommendations for the identification and assessment of children with special educational needs;

(c) to provide advice on strategies for adapting, modifying and supporting the 5–16 curriculum to meet their needs in ordinary schools;

(d) to provide practical classroom orientated advice about meeting special needs in ordinary schools;

(e) to provide guidelines on the working of the Education Act 1981 and the statutory processes involved;

(f) to provide the framework for implementation of a school-based in-service programme on special educational needs;

(g) to provide information on the roles and responsibilities of the support services and how they may be most effectively employed.

The material is produced in seven units covering the development of special education; a whole-school approach; general educational principles; learning difficulties; physical and sensory special needs; emotional, behavioural, cultural and social aspects; post-school education and school-based in-service work. The section on support services is very detailed and directly related to the Essex situation. A strong point of the material is the emphasis on classroom observation and record-keeping which are closely associated in the approach.

Video Observation Material for Teacher Education: Special Educational Needs—Observations of Individual Children

In a different approach, ILEA uses its exceptionally rich educational television facility to provide teachers with observations of pupils that would not otherwise be possible. The material covers needs as described in Chapter 3 of the Warnock Report. Of 24 planned units, 17 are now in use. Each unit concentrates on an individual child engaged in his usual learning activities in their own classroom. Notes present essential background information and a summary of the content material written at tutor/discussion group-leader level, thus facilitating flexible use of the material and assisting analysis of the video-audio sequences.

Examples of the units are as follows.

Wendy: an 8-year-old girl with mild learning difficulties in primary school.
Philip: an 8-year-old boy with emotional difficulty in special school.
Roger: a 12-year-old boy with physical difficulties in secondary school.
Denis: a 16-year-old autistic boy in a special school.
Cathy: a 17-year-old girl with profound and multiple learning difficulties in a
    special school.
Kevin: a 12-year-old boy with emotional difficulties in tutorial class.
Paul: a 12-year-old boy with mild learning difficulties in secondary school.

There are also some group observations:

Maria, Mark, Natasha, Shabaz and Tommy, five 12-year-olds with mild learning
    difficulties in the context of a special needs department of a comprehen-
    sive school at three stages during their first year.
Ibrahim, Jenny and Mark, three pre-school children with special educational
    needs working at home with their teachers and parents.

To put the above material in context there are similar video observations in child
development covering children without special needs, the detailed notes prepared
in collaboration with NFER.
Longitudinal studies are also available:

David: from first hour of birth to 2 years (continuing)
Samantha: from thirteen months to 2 years.
Claire: severe learning difficulties from 3 to 13 years, including school and home
    observations.

Further information from: ILEA, Centre for Learning Resources, 275 Kennington
Lane, London SE11 5QZ.

Teachers of Children with Special Educational Needs (TOCEN)

This one-term full-time course is run twice per year by ILEA. It takes training
beyond basic awareness and allows teachers from primary, secondary and special
schools to work together. It is orientated towards ordinary schools but the detailed
curriculum is under review. A course such as this would lend itself to inter-LEA or
regional cooperation, it appears compatible with the new development in INSET
noted in the text, and it would fit easily into the modular course noted in Appendix
5.

Microelectronics in Special Education

The Microelectronics Education Programme (MEP) terminated in March 1986 and was succeeded by the Microelectronics Support Unit (MESU) which is directed by John Foster and based at the University of Warwick. MESU covers children of school age in England, Wales and Northern Ireland. Scotland having its own programme managed by the Scottish Council for Educational Technology. MESU is to run for five years from March 1986.

MESU is continuing the work of the MEP in special education through its special education section which will continue to be coordinated by Mary Hope from the Council for Educational Technology in London. The plan is that the work of the section will continue for three years by which time it should be firmly established in LEAs, and there will be some support from the central unit for a further two years. Thus the following organizations set up by MEP will continue for three years.

Special Education Microelectronic Resource Centres (SEMERCs)

Bristol SEMERC: Bristol Polytechnic, Redland Hill, Bristol B56 6UZ (0272 733141)
Manchester SEMERC: Manchester Polytechnic, Hathersage Road,
   Manchester M13 0JA (061-225 9054)
Newcastle SEMERC: Newcastle Polytechnic, Coach Lane Campus,
   Newcastle upon Tyne NE7 7XA (0632 665057)
Redbridge SEMERC: Dane Centre, Melbourne Road, Ilford Essex
   (01-478 6363)

Special Needs Software Centre Address as Manchester SEMERC.

Aids for Communication in Education Centre (ACE Centre) Ormerod School, Wayneflete Road, Oxford OX3 8DD. (0865 64508). Specializes in microelectronic aids for children with communication difficulties.

Each SEMERC covers about 25 LEAs and works through a teacher-coordinator in each LEA. They are focal points for information, advice, demonstrations, discussions about microelectronics in special education and repositories for a growing selection of software for examination. Some software may be copied for educational purposes. The software centre has a national responsibility for the production and modification of software to help children with special needs but its resources are limited in relation to the task so priorities have had to be agreed. The focus is on framework programmes that can be easily adapted to meet teachers' needs. Micro-switches, special keyboards, voice synthesizers and portable computers are among the equipment held at ACE Centre and may be tried out by teachers and children. One member of the ACE team is based at the Manchester SEMERC to service the North of the country. See: 'MESU and Children with Special Needs–How it Works and What it Does', *Briefing*, no. 1, July 1986 (copies from LEA Special Needs/Micro-electronic co-ordinators, or from the Council for Educational Technology).

Other Addresses

Microelectronics Support Unit, University of Warwick, Coventry CV4 7AL.
Council for Educational Technology, 3 Devonshire Street, London W1N 2BA.
Scottish Council for Educational Technology, Dowanhill, 74 Victoria Cresent Road, Glasgow G12 9JN.

Scotland and Northern Ireland

The Education Act 1981 and the Regulations arising from it, together with the discussion of detailed procedures in the text, apply to children, parents and schools in England and Wales only. The situations in Scotland and Northern Ireland are regulated by separate legislation for each of the areas. While the legislation establishes duties and rights for parents and education authorities in relation to children with special educational needs that are consistent with those discussed in the text for England and Wales procedures are different and the appropriate legislation must be consulted on all matters of detail.

In Scotland, for instance, the Statement of Special Educational Need becomes a Record of Need, though the content and the sections remain identical; and though the local appeals committee has a function as for England and Wales, its power is significantly extended. In Northern Ireland education is the responsibility of the area Education and Library Board and appeals against board decisions in relation to special educational needs are to the Department of Education, Belfast. At the time of writing the boards are not responsible for severely mentally handicapped children though it is anticipated that they will assume responsibility in April 1987.

Legislation for Scotland.
Education (Scotland) Act, 1981 Sections 3 & 4, Schedules 1, 2 & 3.

Legislation for Northern Ireland.
Education and Libraries (Northern Ireland) Order, 594, 1986.

Further Reading

There is a useful review of the history of special education in Chapter 2 of the *Warnock Report*; for those requiring more detail, the most comprehensive is D. G. Pritchard, *Education and the Handicapped*, Routledge & Kegan Paul, 1963. The legalities are covered comprehensively in the latest edition of Taylor & Saunders, *The Law of Education*, Butterworth, though there is a clear exposition in D. Nice, *Education and the Law*, Longman, 1986. For the 1981 Act and its ramifications, and especially for parents, nothing betters P. Newell, *ACE Special Educational Handbook*, Advisory Centre for Education, 1985, which is of value to anyone looking for a clear account of parental rights. In fact, when looking for clear expositions of legal rights and information on integration of children with special needs in ordinary schools, ACE and CSIE (Centre for Studies on Integration in Education) should be a first reference—for addresses, see Appendix 2. The ACE bi-monthly *ACE Bulletin* is an excellent way to keep abreast of developments. The National Union of Teachers publishes two good short guides on *The Education Act 1981* and *Meeting Special Educational Needs in Ordinary Schools*.

Surveys of special education now tend to be outdated by the recent changes, but for those who want a view of what went before R. Gulliford, *Special Educational Needs*, Routledge & Kegan Paul, 1971, or Younghusband *et al.*, *Living With Handicap*, National Children's Bureau, 1970, offer sound information from the early 1970s. Younghusband *et al.* look forward and offer suggestions for change, but for a look into the future that goes beyond suggestions in this current text, see J. Fish, *Special Education: The Way Ahead*, Open University Press, 1985.

There should shortly be some researched information on the contemporary situation from the projects described in Appendix 5. Meanwhile there are some useful texts available: D. Galloway, *Schools, Pupils and Special Educational Needs*, Croom Helm, 1985, ranges widely over post-Warnock issues and problems; T. Booth and J. Statham eds, *The Nature of Special Education*, Croom Helm and Open University Press, 1982, brings together readings on personalities, perspectives and problems in special education; T. Booth and P. Potts eds, *Integrating Special Education*, Blackwell, 1983, consists of a series of readings pertinent to the title. Two titles by S. Hegarty and K. Polkington, *Educating Pupils with Special Needs in Ordinary Schools*, 1981, and *Integration in Action: Case Studies in the Integration of Pupils with Special Needs*, 1982, both published by NFER-Nelson, offer descriptions and insights based upon organized research. *Educational Opportunities for All* (Fish Report), ILEA, 1986, presents an objective and thorough survey of special education in a large inner-city LEA, identifies strengths and weakness and points the way forward. It has usefulness and implications much wider than the LEA concerned. It will be a long time before *Special Educational Needs* (Warnock Report), HMSO, 1978, is outdated as a source book.

More specific to teaching and curriculum are: R. Gulliford, *Teaching Children With Learning Difficulties*, NFER-Nelson, 1985, which offers a wide-ranging post-Warnock overview of the problem. W. K. Brennan, *Curriculum for Special Needs*, Open University Press, 1985, an examination of problems in incorporating special needs within a common approach to curriculum. A. E. Tansley and R. Gulliford, *The Education of Slow Learning Children*, Routledge & Kegan Paul, 1960, still has much to offer. M. Chazan *et al.*, *Some of Our Children*, Open Books, 1980, concentrates on the early education of children with special needs. M. D. Wilson, *The Curriculum in Special Schools*, Longman for Schools Council, 1981, is the report of a seminar.

The importance of ACE publications for parents has already been noted; other helpful publications are P. Mittler and H. Mittler, *Partnership With Parents*, National Council for Special Education; J. Stone and T. Taylor, *Handbook for Parents with a Handicapped Child*, Arrow, 1977; A. Darnborough & D. Kincade, *Directory for the Disabled*, Woodhead Faulkner in association with Royal Association for Disability and Rehabilitation, 4th edn, 1985; R. Rogers, *Caught in the Act*, CSIE/Spastics Society, 1986; *Integration Information Pack*, CSIE/The Spastics Society; *Guiding Professionals*, CSE/Spastics Society, 1986; *The British Journal of Special Education* (Formerly *Special Education—Forward Trends*), the journal of the National Council for Special Education; *Support for Learning* (Formerly *Remedial Education*), the journal of the National Association for Remedial Education; *Special Children*, an independent monthly magazine for parents, professionals and all interested in children with special needs, established in June 1986 (73 All Saints Road, Kings Heath, Birmingham B14 7LN).

For those interested in continued education the publications of the Further Education Curriculum Review and Development Unit (FEU) are recommended: *A Basis for Choice: Students with Special Needs in Further Education; Stretching the System; Making Progress; Skills for Living; Routes to Coping; Learning for Independence; A College Guide: Meeting Special Educational Needs*. Early titles from FEU; later from Longman Resources Unit, 62 Hallfield Road, Layerthorpe, York YO3 7XQ.

Index